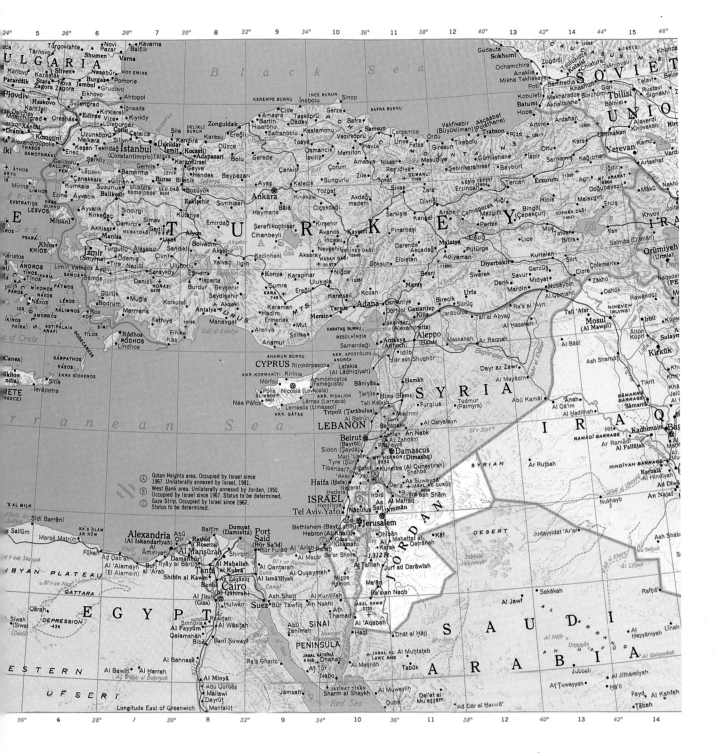

Enchantment of the World

SYRIA

By Margaret Beaton

Consultant for Syria: Bernard Reich, Ph.D., Professor, Department of Political Science, George Washington University, Washington, D.C.

Consultant for Reading: Robert L. Hillerich, Ph.D., Bowling Green State University, Bowling Green, Ohio

CHILDRENS PRESS ®

CHICAGO

Men of Aleppo enjoying their waterpipes

Library of Congress Cataloging-in-Publication Data

Beaton, Margaret.
  Syria / by Margaret Beaton.
     p.   cm. — (Enchantment of the world)
  Includes index.
  Summary: Discusses the geography, history, people,
economy, and customs of the ancient land of Syria.
  ISBN 0-516-02708-5
  1. Syria—Juvenile
literature. [1. Syria.] I. Title. II. Series.
DS93.B43 1988   88-18697
956.91—dc19   CIP
                                              AC

Childrens Press®, Chicago

Picture Acknowledgments
Journalism Services/MARKA: © L. Giaretti: 8, 17, 57 (top right), 106 (top left)
Journalism Services/Imapress: © Gérard Degeorge: 4, 24 (bottom left), 26 (top right), 56 (top right), 61 (bottom right), 106 (top right), 117, 118, 119
© **Photri:** 5, 6, 18, 19, 23 (left), 24, (top & bottom right), 27, 29, 31 (bottom left), 33, 47, 71, 97 (right), 107
Shostal Associates, Inc.: 14, 34 (top), 40; © Kurt Scholz: Cover, 10, 13, 15, 23 (right), 26 (top left), 32, 46, 58 (right), 59, 98 (left), 100 (bottom left); © Charles May: 20; © D. Von Knobloch: 22, 44 (right), 50; © Jill Brown: 28 (left), 34 (bottom), 97 (left), 100 (bottom right); © Nigel Smith: 28 (right), 52 (left), 103 (left); © Giorgio Richtto: 36; © Peter Schmid: 58 (left), 100 (top left); © A.C. Forbes: 100 (top right)
Valan Photos: © C. Osborne: 16 (2 photos), 25 (left), 26 (bottom left & right), 31 (top & bottom right), 44 (left), 48, 51, 53 (3 photos), 55 (left), 56 (top left, bottom left & right), 57 (left), 60 (left), 61 (left & top right), 66 (left), 98 (right), 99, 102 (2 photos), 103 (right), 106 (bottom left)
Root Resources: © Irene Hubbell: 25 right; © Naji M. Al-Hasani: 52 (right), 60 (right), 63
Historical Pictures Service, Chicago: 38, 41, 65, 66 (right), 70 (2 photos), 72 (right)
H. Armstrong Roberts: © G. Tortoti: 54, 55 (right), 104, 106 (bottom right)
H. Armstrong Roberts/Charles Phelps Cushing Collection: 64, 72 (left)
AP/Wide World Photos: 75, 76, 79, 81, 83, 85, 87, 89, 90, 93
Len W. Meents: Maps on pages 20, 29, 31, 76
Courtesy Flag Research Center, Winchester, Massachusetts 01890: Flag on back cover
Cover: Vineyards in Maalula

A typical village, with the mosque's minaret in the foreground

TABLE OF CONTENTS

The street called Straight

Chapter 1

A CROSSROADS OF
HISTORY

This ancient land on the eastern shores of the Mediterranean Sea has been a gateway between Asia, Europe, and Africa for thousands of years. At the very dawn of history, Syria was home to the Babylonian-Mesopotamians who came from the Fertile Crescent between the Tigris and Euphrates rivers. Syria knew the Old Testament Israelites, descendants of the Hebrew patriarch Jacob; the prophet Abraham himself wandered Syria's deserts and rested in its oases. Syria's capital, Damascus, is one of the oldest inhabited cities in the world. It has sheltered Alexander the Great, Salome, John the Baptist, and the apostle Paul, who, according to the New Testament, experienced a revelation "on the road to Damascus" and another in Damascus "on the street called Straight" (Acts 9:11). You still can walk along that street in the old section of Damascus today.

Innumerable people from Europe and Asia have traveled across Syria's camel caravan routes, trading in silks and spices. The great Greek, Roman, and Byzantine empires ruled over Syria. The seventh-century Muslim Empire that ruled from Damascus helped

The Syrian Desert

spread Muslim rule as far east as India and west all the way to Spain and France. Egyptians and Turks ruled Syria for hundreds of years, followed by the British and the French.

Historically, this meeting and mingling of cultures has contributed to many great civilizations. Syria has been able to serve as a bridge between East and West, making possible advances in science, philosophy, art, and commerce. However, this East/West relationship also has produced conflicts and deeply entrenched resentments.

There are historical roots for most of what happens in Syria and the Middle East today. Modern-day Syrians keep abreast of twentieth-century life, but the glories of their past are alive in the memories of the people—and so are the abuses and frustrations of foreign domination. In this tradition-conscious society, current events are often measured in terms of past actions.

Chapter 2

MOUNTAINS, DESERTS, AND CITIES

Inevitably, everything depends first of all on the land. People are dependent on the land for their very survival and will fish, farm, or hunt according to what the land offers. From this, social organization is determined—whether to live in small family groups as farmers or travel in hunting or fishing groups. If there is abundance, a great number of people will want, and be able, to live in one area. If the land is very fertile, many will establish permanent residences and stable institutions. Thus, towns and cities are born.

The life of those who live in deserts is a continual migration to find new sources of water and grass for their animals. This nomadic life—living in tents and having few possessions, not being able to go to school or mosque—is quite different from the life of Syrians who live in farming areas, port towns, or in great, ancient, stable cities, such as Damascus and Aleppo.

More than ten million people live in Syria today. Most of them are concentrated either in the large cities or in the fertile areas, where there is water.

Mountains in the north

Syria encompasses deserts, mountains, and some of the most fertile areas in the Middle East. Syria is not a large country, 71,467 square miles (185,180 square kilometers). It is about the size of the state of North Dakota or twice the size of the country of Portugal.

BORDERS

To the north of Syria lies Turkey, to the east and southeast is Iraq, and Jordan is south. A small area, the Golan Heights, separates Syria from Israel to the southwest. On the west, Syria has a short but important coastline of 94 miles (151 kilometers) on the Mediterranean Sea. South of this coastal area lies Lebanon on Syria's western border. The Anti-Lebanon Mountains running north to south form a natural border between Lebanon and Syria.

CLIMATE

The climate of Syria is hot and dry. There is precious little rain in the desert, but in the coastal area rainfall is sufficient to produce many crops. Even the Syrian Desert is interspersed with grasslands, which unfortunately dry up during the long, hot summer.

Most of the water is provided either by the rivers or by underground springs, which in the desert create oases. But in summer both the smaller rivers and the underground springs either dry up or are exhausted, sometimes very quickly. Then nomads are obliged to seek new wells. The larger rivers, particularly the Euphrates, do not dry up, so year-round cultivation is possible.

GEOGRAPHICAL AREAS

There are several distinct geographical areas in Syria. The coastal area is fertile alluvial plain, thanks to the moisture that comes from the Mediterranean. The Jabal an Nusayriyah mountains serve as a wall that blocks this moisture. The east side of the mountains is quite dry, receiving the hot, dry winds from the desert. This mountain range stretches north to south and separates the coastal plain from the steppe, which is for a while a fertile area, and then becomes desert.

Other fertile areas are found along the rivers—the Euphrates, the Orontes, and the Barada. An aerial view of Syria shows the river areas as they cut through the desert.

A rocky desert fills most of Syria's landmass and supports a very small percentage of the population. Several mountain ranges cross the desert, roughly from the north to the south.

THE SYRIAN DESERT

The geographical desert extends east and south into Iraq and Jordan. Across this great rocky desert, caravans traveled for centuries, navigating sometimes along visible trails, more usually only by stars.

This is not the fine, smooth sand of Saudi Arabia or the Sahara of North Africa, but a rocky desert, with rocks of all kinds—huge boulders, rocks, and small stones. Scrub and coarse grasses are found interspersed in the rocky mountain ranges. But sand there is, nonetheless, among the stones; sand that shifts and changes the topography of the land. At certain times of the year, massive sandstorms that create what seems to be solid walls of sand blow

The Valley of Tombs near the ancient city of Palmyra

across the desert, even into Damascus, which is in a valley oasis on the edge of the Syrian Desert. These sandstorms disrupt life completely until they are over.

Rainfall in the desert is only about 5 inches (12.7 centimeters) a year, compared to 30 to 40 inches (76 to 101.6 centimeters) along the coast. In ancient times, when this area was given the name the Fertile Crescent (which it is still called), a large part of the Syrian Desert benefited from the great fertility of the Tigris and Euphrates rivers and their tributaries that cut through the desert. Due to natural causes this area lost the fertility it had in ancient times and steadily diminished. In the past, too, the Syrian Desert had many oases, around which great cities rose, encouraged by the trade of the caravans that traveled there. The present-day city of Tudmur is one of those ancient oasis-cities, once called Palmyra, at the north edge of the desert. Most of the other oasis cities died when the oases ran dry, others may have been destroyed by hostile tribes.

A nomad crossing the desert

In any event, the desert is an archaeologist's delight. Many of the geographical features, such as mounds, hills, and small rises, cover the ruins of ancient settlements. Many Syrians insist that an archaeologist could start digging almost anywhere and uncover a town or small settlement covered by the sands, or at least discover pieces of pottery. There are certainly more ruins and likely ruins than an archaeologist has time or capabilities to explore. Certainly, treasures from ancient civilizations lie still buried, protected from decay by the dry air.

The only life that is possible in the desert is that of the nomad, who travels with the seasons. Nomads are shepherds. They travel with their camels or sheep, who graze on the rough grasses. In summer, when the dry season occurs, they must move westward. The bedouin live on the desert as they have for thousands of years, dependent primarily on their camel, which they use for milk,

Fertile land along the Euphrates River

occasionally for meat, and for making tents from camel hair. The camel is not necessarily a means of transport, for there is very little to transport. Sometimes, trucks transport the camels.

Few animals except the camel can live on the desert, but there is enough vegetation to support occasional gazelles, as well as rodents, eagles, lizards, and falcons.

The Euphrates River is the most beneficial feature of the vast desert. It is the only navigable river, flowing from Turkey south across Syria to Iraq. The tributaries of this river provide a fertile area, which has undergone numerous improvements, including the huge Tabka Dam, which created the Assad Reservoir and has expanded production of cereals, cotton, and date palms.

Half of the world's oil is found in the Middle East. In the northeast section of Syria, near the border with Turkey, a number of small oil fields were discovered. Production began in 1968 and by 1970, Syria was exporting oil.

Left: The port of Latakia
Above: Women doing their laundry in the Orontes River

THE COAST

This area enjoys a milder climate and more rainfall than the interior. Because of the beneficial moisture and good soil, it is intensely and efficiently cultivated. The temperate climate allows crops to be grown in winter as well as summer. Vegetables and fruits grown here are shipped to other parts of Syria, as well as abroad. Fruit trees are grown easily and oak and poplar grow naturally.

The two major port cities, Latakia and Tartus, transport goods, not just from Syria but the entire area. The immediate coastline is not cultivated, but is lined with numerous sandy bays and rocky cliffs.

In this coastal region, people dress less like traditional desert Arabs. Women tend to wear conservative blouses and skirts and

Beehive-shaped houses of the coastal region

are rarely veiled, but this varies from village to village. Houses are very different from the flat-topped style seen throughout the rest of Syria; they have a very unique beehive shape.

MOUNTAINS

One main mountain range, the Jabal an Nusayriyah, runs north to south along the coastal plain. It is sometimes called Jabal Alawite, because it is the ancient stronghold of the Alawites, a Muslim sect. Agriculture is practiced on the western side, where there is more moisture, but on the eastern side, sheep herding is the only practical endeavor. The Orontes River flows alongside this range on the east, with a kind of corridor next to it called the Ghab Depression. Historically, this has been a convenient route for traders as well as armies.

A fertile valley at the base of the Anti-Lebanon Mountains

To the south, the mountain range continues and is called the Anti-Lebanon Mountains, half of which are on the Lebanese side. While the climate in the mountains is preferable to the desert, it is still an agriculturally poor area. And because of its difficult passage, did not profit from the trade routes in ancient times as the desert area did. The area is favorable for raising sheep, and here are the only real forests in Syria, with yews, fir, and even lime trees, as well as drought-resistant trees such as myrtle, boxwood, and turpentine. While the camel is the beast of burden in the desert, only mules can be used in the mountains.

THE CULTIVATED STEPPE

A steppe is basically a plain—simply a large, flat area. The Syrian steppe begins where the mountains end and extends all

Cultivated mountain slopes

across the desert. The Syrian steppe is essentially arid, but there are fertile areas created by the many rivers that flow down from the mountains. These areas are referred to as the cultivated steppe, because farming is possible. It covers a small, but strategically important, area.

CITIES

Nearly half of Syria's population lives in cities and, similar to many Third World countries, more people are moving into the cities every year. Most of the cities are ancient settlements located at strategic geographic points — on great rivers, in the midst of fertile areas, on the sea, or on trade routes. The cities that rose up on oases when the camel caravans crossed the Syrian Desert died out when the trade did. This occurred around the time that

Aleppo

★ Damascus

Traffic in downtown Damascus

Columbus discovered America, when a new sea route was found around the Cape of Africa to transport goods to and from the Far East. There was no longer any need to take the onerous route across the Syrian Desert. Tudmur is the only major city that remains on the ancient trade route that once had beautiful cities on every oasis, and it is now only a shadow of its former glory.

DAMASCUS

Damascus and Aleppo are the two largest cities, and both are quite ancient. Both date from the third millenium B.C. and they have been rivals for almost that long. Damascus is the larger, with a population of some two million people. It also is better known to Westerners, and its fame in history is quite justified. It was truly a "fabled city" that every conqueror in history considered an important prize worth risking life and limb to possess. It was a magnet that attracted the wealthy, the wise, the ingenious, the religious—and the ambitious. It attracted also the poor who fled the desert in times of drought, and Damascus sustained them, too.

Damascus is nestled at the foot of the Anti-Lebanon Mountains. It has an average rainfall of 7 inches (17.7 centimeters), more moisture than the desert to the east, but a good deal less than Beirut, Lebanon, just 50 miles (80 kilometers) away, which has over 33 inches (83.8 centimeters) of rain a year. Damascus's great advantage is that it is in a fertile area so close to the desert. It was the last place traders could stop and refuel and purchase provisions for their long trip, and it was the first stop on their return from the trip across the desert. Damascus was built on trade, and this provided a solid base on which to build many other kinds of commerce.

Today Damascus is still an important crossroads for trade between Baghdad, Iraq; Beirut, Lebanon; and Amman, Jordan; as well as Kuwait and all the countries of the Arabian Peninsula. This is due in part to its location, but also because of the capabilities, both physical and human, that Damascus has acquired over time.

During the rainy winter season from November to February, rain fills wells and rivers in the Damascus area. Winter is temperate, but occasionally the temperature falls below freezing. Spring is remarkably beautiful, with pink flowering almond trees and jasmine flowers in full bloom that also lend their sweet perfume to the air. But spring lasts for a short period in March and April. In May, the beautiful flowers and grasses dry up and only the scrub plants survive as spring changes into summer. Summer lasts quite a long time, with August the hottest month;

Olive pickers

temperatures average about 80 degrees Fahrenheit (26.7 degrees Celsius) and sometimes reach 111 degrees Fahrenheit (43.9 degrees Celsius).

Desert oases are most often formed by underground springs that reach the surface in small pools. In the case of the Ghutah Oasis, where Damascus is situated, the water comes from the Barada River that flows down from the Anti-Lebanon Mountains and slowly trails off and dries up in the desert. In summer, the nomads are obliged to come closer and closer to Damascus and its precious water, (but could not possibly cross the mountains to the water on the other side).

Thanks to the Barada River, trees such as oak, poplar, and aspen grow naturally along its banks. But the main feature of the area is the many orchards. Apricot, peach, apple, nut, and olive trees are here in abundance, giving it truly the appearance of a biblical

Above: The tomb of Saladin
Left: Omayyad Mosque

Garden of Eden. The orchards are cultivated and must be irrigated
in dry months with water from the river or wells.

Rainfall in the area is variable. Sometimes the Barada River
floods to the size of a long lake, after a rainfall of 13 or 14 inches
(33 to 35 centimeters). In other years, rainfall can be as little as 6
inches (15.2 centimeters), and during a drought in 1959-60,
rainfall was only 2 inches (5 centimeters).

In 1932 a water-supply system was built that provided running
water through the city by way of underground canals, drawing
this water from a source of the Barada River. Sewage is discharged
into rivers and streams farther away.

Damascus is continually growing and is surrounded by
suburbs. Damascus itself has separate residential, commercial, and
industrial zones. The Great Mosque, the tomb of Saladin, and the
Mosque of Sultan Suleiman are excellent examples of Islamic

Above: Almerje Plaza, Damascus
Below Right: Part of the bazaar in the
Old City of Damascus
Below Left: A vendor selling tamarind juice

The Aleppo-Damascus highway (left) and a man selling vegetables from his donkey-powered cart (right)

architecture. Despite the numerous times Damascus has been destroyed, a great number of ancient buildings can still be found. Theaters and museums, plus the National Library and the University of Damascus add to the culture of the city.

Tall modern buildings with balconies built of reinforced concrete are numerous. Many people complain that these modern buildings are intolerably hot in summer and prefer the old low style of building that has existed in the area for hundreds of years, with thick walls and an inner court. But these no longer are being built and are found only in the Old City.

Also in the Old City are the bazaars, or *souks*, where merchants market their goods and craftsmen sell fabrics and metalware, as they have done for centuries.

ALEPPO

Syria's second-largest city, with a population of nearly two million, is not as well known to Westerners, even though Aleppo has been around for as long as Damascus. At many times in its history, it eclipsed Damascus as a commercial, cultural, and political center.

Scenes of Aleppo, clockwise from top left, include
the entrance to the National Museum, remains of the citadel,
a residential area, and a street vendor selling cheese.

A panoramic view of Aleppo

At first glance, it may not be apparent from Aleppo's geographical position why and how it was able to grow to such greatness. The area is relatively dry with about 18 inches (45.7 centimeters) of rain per year. There is no major river or seaport nearby, except for the small stream, the Quwayq. However, it is situated on an ancient trade route between the Euphrates River and the Mediterranean Sea, and that was certainly an important factor. But Aleppo's big geographical advantage was its impregnability. It is situated on a rocky elevation that protected it from hostile tribes. Here people could be secure and civilization could thrive. Original fortifications were built and rebuilt by succeeding cultures, including the Greeks and the Umayyad and Ayyubid dynasties, or *caliphates.*

A great citadel from the thirteenth century is still in fine condition and near it is the Umayyad Great Mosque. Archaeological material found at ancient sites are displayed in the

A tractor factory in Aleppo (left) and Muslim women harvesting irrigated squash (right)

National Museum. The city has several Muslim theological schools, a university, and an institute of music.

Aleppo itself is now the most industrialized city in Syria, with silk weaving and cotton printing its main industries. Other industries also draw on the natural products from the surrounding area, such as tanning animal hides and processing produce. Although Aleppo is set on rocks, the area around Aleppo is very fertile, with heavy cultivation of wheat, barley, fruit, and nuts.

LATAKIA

Latakia is Syria's main port. With a population of a little over 200,000 people, it is a good deal smaller than Damascus and Aleppo. It is situated on a fine harbor on the Mediterranean Sea, surrounded by fertile land. People have lived here since the twelfth century B.C., and, like Aleppo, Latakia has had a strong Greek influence. Latakia has known some catastrophic earthquakes in ancient times that destroyed it, except for a Roman triumphal arch and Corinthian columns. The university, called Tishrin University, was founded in 1971.

Boats in Latakia, the main port of Syria

Everything seems to flourish in the fertile area around Latakia, and this bounty—fruits, cereals, tobacco, cotton, vegetable oil, and eggs—is easily exported to other less fertile countries in the region.

HOMS

Situated in the center of a desert area, Homs is near the great Orontes River, which provides water to irrigate a significant sector of fertile land that runs along the river. The Orontes River begins in the mountains of Lebanon near Baalbek. A dam (now called Lake Qattine) which dates back to the second millenium B.C. lies just south of Homs and supplies Homs with all of its water for drinking and for irrigation.

Historically Homs has been a distribution center for produce grown in the region and it has been famous for its fine handicrafts. In 1959 an oil refinery added a new dimension to Homs's importance. In addition, several oil pipelines were built to transport oil from Iraq, and they cross at Homs. Important railways and roads cross at Homs, too, linking the interior with the Mediterranean Sea. Homs is larger than Latakia, with over 300,000 people.

HAMA

The Orontes River flows through the center of Hama. Trees, gardens, and ancient waterwheels, called *norias*, line the riverbanks. These waterwheels were built centuries ago to bring water to the town. Although they are necessary no longer, they still churn and people come to rest and cool off nearby.

Top: *The city of Hama*
Above: *Plowing the land near Homs*
Left: *A noria, an ancient waterwheel, in Hama*

Roman ruins from the third century

Excavations have uncovered temples and colonnades from ancient Palmyra.

TUDMUR

Tudmur, formerly Palmyra, is one of the most famous historical sites in the world. At one time, Palmyra was an important oasis for caravans traveling across the desert, as far back as the times of Marco Polo. In the first century A.D., Romans conquered the city and in 217 it became a Roman colony. In the 600s, the Muslims ruled and then in 1089, an earthquake completely destroyed the city. In 1924, excavations began and many ruins, such as temples, colonnades, theaters, and marketplaces, have been uncovered.

Two interior views of Omayyad Mosque in Damascus, where Muslims worship.

Chapter 3

RELIGION

RELIGION AS A PART OF EVERYDAY LIFE

While Islam is not the only religion practiced in Syria, it is the
dominant one. It is the single greatest influence in Syria because
Islam extends to every area of life, officially and unofficially,
philosophically, spiritually, and practically. Islam affects law and
is a major factor in modern politics. Islam even has its own laws
and courts.

When Syria became an independent, self-governing state,
Islamic ideals and laws were incorporated into the law of the land.
Although Syria is not as strict an Islamic state as some others,
such as Saudi Arabia, Iran, Iraq, or even Morocco, the constitution
does specify that the laws of the country must be based on Islamic
law and that the president of Syria must be a Muslim. Nonetheless
the constitution guarantees religious freedom.

The religious sects are self-contained communities. They can be
thought of as large support groups or networks. The reasons for
this lie in part in history. In the hundreds of years under foreign

Muslims washing their feet before entering the mosque

rulers, Syrians found they could not count on a foreign
government for help or redress of certain grievances, so they
developed their own systems. Syrians depended on their own
families, kinsmen, and religious communities and developed
feudal-style loyalties within them.

About 86 percent of Syrians are Muslims. Of these, about 75
percent are Sunnis. The second largest group are Alawites and the
third largest are Druzes, which are both offshoots of Shiite Islam.
Christians comprise about 10 percent of the population. They are
Arabs or Armenians whose Christian tradition dates back to the
time of Christ and his apostles. The principal Christian churches
include the Syrian Orthodox, Greek Orthodox, and Armenian
Orthodox. A few thousand Jews live in Syria, but the majority
have emigrated to Israel and their number is dwindling.

ISLAM

Because Islam is so important in Syria, a closer look at the Muslim faith and its sects will tell us a great deal about the Syrians and their outlook on life, as well as the organization of Syrian society.

As in any society, attitudes to religion differ. Some people are profoundly religious, some a little religious, and others not religious at all, or are even very cynical about religion. It is the same in Syria. But even those Muslims who are not religious still identify themselves as Muslims and are members of specific sects. But there are a great many Syrians who are very religious and who take their faith seriously. For these people Islam provides a reassuring rule of conduct for every area of life and also a satisfying spiritual experience.

MUHAMMAD, THE FOUNDER OF ISLAM

All Muslims recognize Muhammad as the founder and prophet of Islam. According to standard doctrine, he is not divine (as Christians believe Jesus was); Muslims recognize only God as divine. Muhammad was one of many prophets, starting with Moses, including Jesus, and ending with Muhammad, who is for Muslims the greatest prophet.

At the time that Muhammad lived, in the sixth and seventh centuries A.D., the Arabs of Arabia, where he lived, and in the Middle East and North Africa, practiced a variety of pagan religions, worshiping animal gods or natural elements, such as the sun. These religions varied from area to area, with each tribe often having its own special deities. Often, when one tribe conquered

Muhammad, the founder of Islam

another, they would force the conquered tribe to accept new gods. These people had been exposed to the monotheistic beliefs of the Jews who lived in the area, and the Christians had tried to convert them, but without success.

According to Islamic teaching, Muhammad had a series of revelations from the angel Gabriel (who is mentioned in the Old Testament of the Bible), telling him to worship the "one true God." Muhammad was overwhelmed by this experience and was inspired to bring the truth of his revelations to the pagans of the area.

The Arabic word for god is "Allah." Allah is not a different God from the Judeo-Christian religion, but the same. And the God that the angel Gabriel revealed was the God of Abraham, Isaac, and Jacob. The angel told Muhammad he was to be the "Messenger of God" by spreading the word of Islam.

THE SCHISM

Muhammad drew a group of followers, who expanded in number. They formed an army and invaded nearby areas, where Muhammad's followers continued to grow. After Muhammad died his followers continued in his belief. One of them (called a *caliph*) took over leadership of the community of believers, and when he died, another followed as caliph. The third caliph was assassinated, and the fourth caliph, Muhammad's son-in-law, Ali, was assassinated also. At this point the followers of Muhammad divided in a bitter, violent disagreement. The followers of Ali, who believed that Ali was the true successor to Muhammad, are called Shiites (after *Shiat Ali*, followers of Ali). The others are known as Sunni, meaning orthodox. Within both groups there are divisions based on alternative interpretation of the theology, history, and traditions of Islam.

Over time, separate theologies evolved, as has happened in other religions. In the Arab world today, most Muslims are Sunnis. The largest minority are the Shiites with various minor sects.

UNIVERSAL MUSLIM BELIEFS

Despite differences among sects, there is a firm core of beliefs that is basic to all Muslims.

First of all is "submission to Allah," which is what Islam means in Arabic. Muslim means "one who submits to Allah." Submission is in all ways, to everything, because God is everywhere. God does not reside in any one place, thing, or person.

*The courtyard
of Omayyad Mosque
in Aleppo*

Because there is but one God, no one but God is divine, not
even Muhammad. Muslims reject the Christian belief of a divine
trinity, but they accept Jesus as a prophet, and believe that he did
rise from the dead and ascend into heaven; they also believe that
Muhammad rose from the dead and ascended to heaven. Jesus
was a great prophet, but Muhammad was the greatest and last of
the prophets. Muslims accept the teachings of the Old Testament,
the teachings of Jesus, as well as other religions, including some
Hindu and Zoroastrian beliefs. Muslims believe that God sent
prophets into all lands, at all times.

Beside a Muslim's relation to God, Islam emphasizes a person's
relations with others. Fairness, generosity, and honesty must be
cultivated. Pride is considered a great sin—Muslims bow deeply
when they pray—and greed is another. From these ideals come
laws regarding usury that regulate business and banking in some
Islamic cultures. Adultery is another major sin, and this is one
reason why women are kept separated from men—to avoid
temptation.

A part of the Koran, the Muslims' sacred book

THE FIVE PILLARS OF FAITH

A Muslim has certain duties. Most important is that all Muslims must recite the *shahada*: "There is no god but God, and Muhammad is his Prophet." They must pray five times a day; give alms; fast during the Islamic month of Ramadan; and make a pilgrimage to Mecca once in a lifetime. Obviously, this is not possible for the very poor, but many Muslims try.

THE KORAN

The Koran is the Muslim Bible. It contains the teachings of Muhammad, as his followers remembered them and told them to others, and then wrote them down. It relates the series of revelations that were given to Muhammad by the angel Gabriel, which is why Muhammad is the "messenger" of God.

The Koran is especially revered for being the message of God, through Gabriel, through Muhammad, to ordinary people. Also, at a time when few could read or write, the Koran appeared to be a magical, mysterious emissary. Today the Koran is read or recited in the mosques, and studied by Muslim scholars.

MUSLIM SECTS AND SOCIAL GROUPINGS

Sunni means "orthodox," or "traditional" in Arabic. Sunnis have not embellished the religious principles of basic Islamic belief. But they believe in the authority of the religious community to arrive at a consensus regarding how Islam should be applied and interpreted. Each Sunni Muslim has a direct relationship with God. This is different from the Shiites, who believe that the *imam*, a divinely appointed successor of Muhammad, can make decisions and is infallible. Because Ali had no descendants, their imams are not direct descendants of Ali, but the new imams must be related to previous imams of the past.

Sunnis are somewhat more pragmatic than Shiites. Some Sunnis are quite strict and conservative, while others are modern, liberal, and tolerant. Sunnis are the majority in most of the Muslim world, including Turkey, Egypt, and Iraq, as well as Syria. In Syria they also have been the wealthiest, best educated, and most powerful. They tend to live in cities.

Sunnis have had power in Syria for quite a long time, starting with the Umayyad Caliphate in the seventh century to the Turkish rule that ended in the twentieth century.

The Shiites often have been persecuted, and they believe in the necessity of martyrdom and suffering — they consider Ali a martyr. They are considered fundamentalists and during religious observances have engaged in public displays where they beat themselves with chains.

Shiites are a majority in Iran, but generally are a minority in most other Muslim countries, including Lebanon, Syria's neighbor. They are mainly rural and quite poor. Like most rural people in the Middle East, they are poorly educated. In the past, they have had virtually no political power, compared to the Sunnis, and now, compared to the Alawites.

Alawites are a subsect of the Shiites. They are very secretive about their practices and are considered heretics by some Muslims, mainly because of their strong belief in a divine trinity of Muhammad, Ali, and a Persian named Salman. Alawites are Syria's second-largest group of Muslims and are concentrated along the coast and in neighboring mountains. Although a great many Alawites have risen in the military with the help of President Assad, most other Alawites remain poor and rural.

Druzes are the third-largest Muslim group in Syria. They take their name from an Iranian mystic, but recognize Jethro, from the Old Testament, as their main prophet. They also have a special reverence for Abel who was slain by his brother Cain. Like the Alawites, they are very secretive. Only a Druze knows fully what the Druzes believe. They live in the cities of Damascus, Aleppo, and el-Qunaytijah, and in the southwest mountains known as the Jabal Druze. Druzes are found also in Lebanon and in Israel. (Druzes have served in both the Israeli and Syrian armies.)

SYRIAN CHRISTIANS

The Christians in Syria, although small in number, have had a significant influence on events, and often have important

Christian institutions in Syria include a monastery (left) and the Convent of Taqla (right).

positions in government. This is mainly because they are educated
city dwellers. They are numerous in and around Damascus,
Aleppo, Hama, and Latakia.

Also, Syrian Christians did not convert to a foreigner's religion,
but have been Christians since the beginning of Christianity. They
are quite proud of their Arabic heritage, too. This pride in their
Arabic heritage is growing and many who had Western names are
changing them to Arabic names.

The foreign names of the Christian churches refer to the
language of the liturgy, not to the ethnic makeup: the Greek
Orthodox church uses Greek and Arabic in the services, the Greek
Catholic church uses Greek and Arabic, the Syrian Orthodox and
Syrian Catholic use Syriac in services. But they are all Arabs,
except for the Armenian Orthodox members.

Chapter 4

THE PEOPLE AND
EVERYDAY LIFE

EVERYDAY LIFE

Everyday life for a Syrian nomad living in the desert is quite different from that of a technician or office worker living in an apartment building in Damascus, Aleppo, or Homs. It also is different according to religious customs, wealth, or education.

ARABS

Syrians call themselves Arabs, which is in a general sense just a handy term referring to the language they speak—Arabic. But strictly speaking, Arab refers to origins as Semitic tribes who came up from Arabia. Many northern tribes contributed to the Syrian mixture of tribes, too. The ancient tribal names of Syrian ancestors are Aramaens, Chaldeans, Canaanites, and Assyrians.

About 70 percent of Syrians are classified as "Arabs." The

A road built by the ancient Romans is intact today.

people of Syria have not intermingled with other groups very much. The long occupation of Greeks, Romans, and Turks did not affect the ethnic makeup of the Syrians very much. For Syria is not, and has not been, an "open" society. As in many Muslim countries, people are very private, even secret, and family-oriented.

KURDS

Other than the major Arabic group, there are various distinct minorities, distinguishable by their race, language, or religion. The Kurds are an extremely independent and mostly nomadic people. They often do not consider themselves Syrian, but only Kurds. They live in the Soviet Union, Turkey, Iran, and Iraq, as well as in northern Syria. This area is informally and traditionally called Kurdistan. Other Kurds have given up the nomadic life and have integrated into Syrian society and live in towns. They speak Kurdish, an Iranian language, and tend to be Sunni Muslims.

An Assyrian bas-relief from the ninth century B.C.

ASSYRIANS

The Assyrians are a tribe of northern Syria who were a distinct cultural group for many centuries, but have been integrating into Syrian society little by little. Their language, Syriac, once a very important Semitic language, is becoming obsolete.

ARMENIANS

The country that once was Armenia is now partly in the Soviet Union, where it is called the Armenian Soviet Socialist Republic, partly in Turkey, and partly in Iran. In the nineteenth century, the Turks engaged in a large-scale massacre of the Armenian people. Many Armenians found refuge in Syria and Lebanon.

Armenians speak Armenian, an Indo-European language, and are usually city dwellers who speak fluent Arabic. They are Christians and belong to the Armenian Orthodox church.

Syrian Christians and Muslims live peaceably together. In the northeast, a convent (on the top of the hill) and a mosque (in the foreground) are found close to each other in the same city.

CHRISTIANS AND JEWS

The Christians in Syria are Arabs, of exactly the same extraction as other Syrians. Their ancestors have always lived in Syria. When Islam first came to Syria, most Syrians were Christians, although in a few centuries, conversion to Islam was widespread. Many Syrian Christians retained their religion. In contrast to Lebanon, Christian relations with Muslim groups seem to be peaceful and stable, mainly because they are loyal to Syria and proud of their Arabic heritage.

The Jews, too, are not immigrants, but have made their home in Syria for hundreds, if not thousands, of years. They, too, have Semitic origins. Syria's wars with Israel have created an uncomfortable situation for the Jews in Syria, and while many did not make any effort to leave at the beginning of the conflicts, gradually the numbers of Jews in Syria has grown smaller, most emigrating to Israel.

LIFE-STYLES—THE DESERT NOMADS

Desert life in Syria is most unusual and dramatic to Westerners. But surprisingly, it is also a very romantic idea for Syrians who live in cities, too. If one tends to think of "Arabs" in long, flowing robes, riding on camels, and living in tents on deserts and oases—so do the urbanized Syrians.

Even Syrians who have lived in settled coastal areas and in great cities for hundreds of years, think of the typical "Arab" as a desert dweller. They are proud of that "rough and ready" image, much as Americans might enjoy thinking of themselves as cowboys. Syrians know that their roots are in the desert. The desert life is seen as imparting virtues of character and self-reliance, and it has been somewhat of a custom to send children to live for a while with families in the desert, much as American children are sent off to camp in summer.

BEDOUIN

The bedouin typically live as nomads in the desert. Their life-style, their language, their laws, are the same as they have been for hundreds of years. They speak the purest, oldest form of Arabic, the closest to classical Arabic.

Even though educated city people may decry the bedouin's primitiveness, unruliness, and lack of education, they admire the bedouin for being the purest example of their race, embodying qualities of generosity, hospitality, honor, and—above all—dignity. And they have sympathy for the bedouin's feelings, such as vengefulness and preference for leisure over hard work.

Migrating bedouin

The bedouin are Sunni Muslims, orthodox and traditional. They live by Islamic law and their own tribal laws and have typically ignored all other laws that city dwellers and foreign rulers tried to impose on them.

Bedouin are shepherds of the desert and may keep camel or sheep. Their animals are their source of nourishment and income, and even their tents are made of either camel or sheep hair. There are about eight main hereditary bedouin tribes, but they live in quite small groups, only about five or six tents in a group. Tents are divided into two sections, one for the men and one for the women. Food choice is limited, with cheese, yogurt, bread, coffee, and staples. Meat is eaten rarely, and at such times, it is usually one of their own animals, slaughtered, for a special occasion, such as a wedding or particular feast.

The bedouin migrate into the desert in the rainy winter months, then drive their herds back to the fertile steppe in summer.

Bedouin milking sheep

Actually, the distinction between town and desert people is not always very exact. When the desert becomes overpopulated or there has been severe drought, the nomads must move to the cities and find work. When there is no work in the cities, they must return to the desert to eke out a living as best they can.

The interior of an urban home (left) and the shaded courtyard of another (right)

URBAN LIFE

The wealthier, better-educated Syrians live in a fairly modern style, similar to people in Greece, Italy, or Egypt. Conveniences such as air conditioners are extremely rare, but televisions and radios are common except among the extremely poor. Although television is censored by the government, everyone watches it, and many American programs are shown.

The life-style of less wealthy townspeople is similar to the nomad in many ways. The interior of many houses shows the same rugs and weavings, and mattresses on the floor often replace beds or sofas. As in the desert, the men visit in one room, the women in another, although they may eat together. Customs and

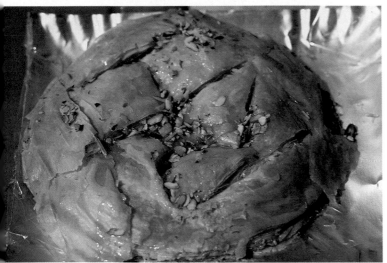

Top left: Kibbeh *is a favorite food in Arab countries. It is made from lamb and bulgur wheat.*
Left: Nahash, *a special pastry for Ramadan*
Above: A pastry shop in Aleppo

etiquette differ from family to family and region to region, but a water pitcher and towel are always offered for washing before and after meals, because fingers rather than utensils are used for eating. A typical meal might consist of flat Syrian bread, meat roasted or broiled with olive oil and lemon, and various dishes made with eggplant, accompanied by cheese, dates, or rose marmalade.

Towns and cities are a blend of old and new, East and West. Much of Damascus and Aleppo are new and modern, but there are old sections with narrow streets and bazaars, where everything looks just as it has for many hundreds of years. Walls of the older houses are very thick to protect against the heat, and often have inner courtyards with gardens.

A family from the north

SOCIAL LIFE

Syrians are warm and friendly, and socializing with family and friends is perhaps the biggest pastime. Like all Mediterraneans, Syrian men like to sit in cafes and talk, aimlessly and endlessly, often about politics. Women do a great deal of socializing, but they are not as visible; they prefer to visit in private homes. Entertaining family and friends in one's home is highly important and extremely enjoyable. Syrian men are very emotional and expressive with people they are close to, and they express affection in public places, but women are more circumspect in public.

The family is most important and always at the center of everything. Individual concerns rarely come ahead of the welfare of the family group. Marriages still are arranged, although these

Left: Friends pass the time in a traditional coffeehouse
Right: The interior of a farmer's house

days it is usually with the bride's consent, and a marriage contract specifies what will happen in case of divorce. If there is a divorce, a woman is always welcome to return to her father's house, because in a sense she never leaves her own family. Blood ties are often stronger than love or marriage. Marriage often creates divided loyalties that can complicate the near-feudal family loyalties. So, many prefer to marry within their own family lineage, although this custom is not observed by Syrian Christians.

WOMEN

Women received the right to vote in the 1960s. With independence and a Socialist regime, there has been a great emphasis on improving conditions for women and giving them

Clockwise from top left: Children in Western dress at the harbor; women, some
carrying bundles on their heads, at a souk; veiled women with their children in Hama;
and shoppers entering and leaving the Old Souk in Aleppo

*A Syrian youth on his motorcycle (left) and a man
(right) wearing an agal to secure his headdress*

more legal rights. There are a fair number of women doctors,
lawyers, teachers, engineers, and a growing number of
politicians—a recent minister of culture was a woman. But these
women belong to the wealthier classes and the condition of poor
women has not shown a great deal of improvement.

DRESS

Customs vary according to religious sect, family custom, and
region. Younger women have greater freedom of dress and life-
style, but the older or traditional women—and there are many—
wear robes in the street, under which nevertheless they may wear
very fashionable dresses. Many, if not most, Syrian women cover
their hair, but very few cover their faces with veils. But in certain
areas, it is a sign of wealth and status to have the women in a
family veiled.

Some men and boys wear jeans and shirts, others wear full-
length tunics and the fabric headdress held on by a black crown
called an *agal* that is a typical Middle Eastern Arabic costume.

Left: An elementary school at an agricultural cooperative near Latakia
Right: Damascus schoolgirls in uniforms

EDUCATION

For all Syrians, education is free and compulsory from six years old up to age eleven. Boys and girls are separated, except at universities. As in many countries, children are put into tracts: if they do not perform well enough, they cannot study certain subjects, and a career as a professional or even a white-collar worker is decided at an early age.

Education is very authoritarian, probably due to the Islamic influence, and children must respect their teachers and professors.They are not encouraged to criticize or challenge teachers. Some feel this attitude impedes the vitality of education,

A popular leisure-time activity is playing dominoes.

particularly at the university level. There are universities at Damascus, Aleppo, Latakia, and Homs.

Literacy rates are improving, particularly among women. But with education compulsory only until age eleven, many people do not bother to read after they leave school and thus do not progress; and very often, people actually forget how to read. There are many newspapers, read mostly by the men. Arabic is considered to be a difficult language to read.

CULTURE AND LEISURE

There are not many books published in Syria, because people still prefer to talk rather than to read. Poetry is important, but it is transmitted mostly through words set to music. Music and folk dancing are an essential part of celebrations, particularly weddings. In some areas men and women dance together, in others they dance separately.

*Left: The intricate artwork on the Treasury
of the Omayyad Mosque
Above: An inscription over the door of
the Aleppo citadel typical of the art form of calligraphy.
Opposite page, clockwise from left: A trader
selling hand-woven blankets, two boys playing
chess, and an artisan working on copper bowls*

The Islamic custom of forbidding any representation of people or animals in "graven images" has had an effect on art forms. Long ago, Syrian artists produced beautiful miniatures in the Persian and Indian styles and before that, in ancient times, Syrians carved beautiful reliefs in stone, similar to the Egyptians.

But under Islamic influence, art became mostly decorative, using geometric designs or flowers carved or painted on walls, and also found in fabrics and rugs. Words themselves have become the highly developed art form of calligraphy.

As in so many other countries, people in cities have greater access to leisure activities than those in small towns. In Damascus there is quite a wide range of pursuits. Many movie theaters show films not only from other Arab countries but from the United States, Europe, India, and Pakistan as well. Alcohol is not

forbidden in Syria and is served at the many night clubs and discotheques frequented by young men and women who lead a very Western life-style. During an important international trade fair held every autumn in Damascus, drawing up to one million participants, the clubs draw large crowds from all over the Middle East.

Soccer, called football, and basketball are very popular in Damascus and there is also wrestling, boxing, and tennis. Thanks to its abundant water sources, Damascus has many swimming pools. To avoid the suffocating heat that lasts most of the year, socializing and most activities tend to be in the cool morning until about 10:00 A.M., and resumes at about 5:00 P.M., and may continue past midnight.

Chapter 5
THOUSANDS OF
YEARS OF HISTORY

Historically "Syria" has referred to a general area that includes present-day Syria, Lebanon, Jordan, Israel, and part of Turkey. This historic or geographic Syria is often called "Greater Syria" to distinguish it from present-day Syria. In fact, the Arab people of the Middle East generally have shared a common history, with the same rulers and the same enemies and heroes, and have developed a sense of kinship that exists to this day—despite separate, autonomous governments.

Syrians live with the visible reminders of their ancient past. Ruins of buildings, temples, and entire towns thousands of years old can be found all across Syria. Many more are still buried under desert sands. The ruins and the tablets that archaeologists have recovered and deciphered tell a story of a long succession of different tribes or city kingdoms that rose, prospered, and declined or were conquered by other tribes.

EARLY SYRIANS

The first Syrians were Semites—nomadic people originally from the area that is Saudi Arabia today—who settled in a broad area

A view of the excavations at Ebla

stretching from the Mediterranean Sea to Babylon (in Iraq) in about 3000 B.C. Archaeologists have found traces of an elaborate, powerful civilization that existed around 2600 B.C. at Ebla. These people traded and warred with other Semitic tribes, and with Egyptians from the south, Hittites from Turkey in the north, and Babylonians to the east.

Other people inhabiting Syria around this time were the Akkadians, Canaanites, and the seafaring Phoenicians who settled along the Mediterranean coast.

At Tell Leilan in the northeast, near the Turkish border, archaeologists have found remains of a civilization believed to have controlled an empire that ruled this area during the end of the eighteenth century B.C. Clay tablets inscribed with cuneiform, an ancient wedge-shaped system of writing, have been found. The tablets were used for correspondence and record keeping. Scribes made impressions with a stylus, a pen-shaped instrument, in wet clay. A seal of the king or royal minister was then pressed into the clay with a rolling cylinder. Then the clay was baked in the sun. If the sender wanted the message to be private, the tablet would be enclosed in more clay that acted as an envelope.

The walls of ancient Jerusalem, overlooking the Mount of Olives

The Aramaens, another Semitic group, established a strong civilization in the center and north by 1500 B.C. Their language, Aramaic, came to dominate Syria, and lasted until the Muslim conquest in the seventh century A.D. Jesus spoke the Aramaic language, and it was still spoken in some Syrian villages in the twentieth century.

In the late 1200s B.C., the Hebrews or Israelites, the world's first monotheistic people, began to migrate into southern Syria. Under King David, they established a kingdom with the capital at Jerusalem, set on a hill west of the Jordan River.

The Aramaens, meanwhile, were creating a strong kingdom whose biblical name was Aram. Their capital was to the north at Damascus, in the valley of an oasis on the edge of the Syrian Desert by the Barada River. The wars between the Damascene Aramaens and the Jersualem Israelites are related in many parts of the Old Testament.

Both lost territories to the Assyrians—Aryans from the north— around 732 B.C., who then were conquered by the Chaldeans in 572 B.C.

In 538 B.C. the great Persian Empire (Persia is now called Iran) defeated the Chaldeans, and Syria became part of the Persian

Alexander the Great and his teacher, Aristotle

Empire until the third century B.C. In the third century, the Persians were conquered by Alexander the Great with his Greek and Macedonian armies.

THE GREEKS

With Alexander's conquest, Syria began to fulfill its destiny as a crossroads and bridge between East and West. Alexander's successors, the Seleucid clan, brought sweeping changes to Syria. Great numbers of Greeks settled in Syria and established widespread trade with India and China that resulted in prosperity for both Greeks and Syrians. The Greeks introduced the teachings of Aristotle and brought literally all of Greek learning to Syria. It was a great revelation to Syrian scholars and many embraced the new learning of Aristotle wholeheartedly. Greek civilization in turn was influenced by Eastern art, philosophy, and science. The unique hybrid of Eastern-influenced Greek culture that resulted was called Near East Hellenism. Under Greek rule, Syrian city-states, such as Damascus and Aleppo, were allowed some freedom to govern themselves, a practice that continued under Roman rule.

Left: Roman fortifications at Busra ash Sham
Right: An artist's version of Roman Emperor Constantine becoming a Christian

THE ROMANS

The Romans took over the area in 64 B.C. The Roman Emperor Hadrian set up a tax system and built roads and aqueducts, all of which are still in use today. The Romans also improved agricultural methods and, although Syria was still under foreign domination, prosperity and progress continued.

CHRISTIANITY

In A.D. 324, the Roman Emperor Constantine became a Christian. He established a Christianized Roman Empire at Byzantium, which he renamed Constantinople after himself (this city is now Istanbul, in Turkey). This Eastern and Christian-influenced Greco-Roman culture was called Byzantine, after Byzantium, Constantinople's former name.

Syrians in the north, nearer to Constantinople, began to convert to Christianity. The most powerful families in Syria tended to be indigenous Syrians who were Christian and who had strong financial and ideological ties to the Byzantine Empire. However, tribes in the countryside, in the south, and the poorer majority tended not to be Christian, but kept to their local, pagan religions.

MUSLIM EMPIRES

Islam spread to Syria just after Muhammad's death in 632. Islam was spread ''by word and by sword'' as conquering armies from Arabia captured Damascus in 635. The Muslim conquest of Syria was a major turning point in Syria's destiny for several reasons. Even though both Christians and Jews had been monotheistic for quite some time—the Jews for thousands of years—many other Syrians worshiped many different deities. With Islam, the tribes were united by a common belief in one god who cared for them all equally. Furthermore, the same Islamic laws governed most aspects of life. And gradually Syrians came to speak Arabic, the language of Muhammad, and the language in which the Muslim's holy book, the Koran, is written.

UMAYYAD CALIPHATE

Great progress in many areas followed the Islamic conquest. The Umayyad family established a ruling caliphate in Syria in 661.

They chose Damascus as their capital. From there they began to fight for the propagation of Islam. They were responsible for the conquest of lands in the name of Islam as far east as India, westward along the north of Africa, and then north across the Mediterranean Sea to Spain and the south of France. Their empire was larger than any Greek or Roman empire at its height.

The Umayyads were talented and energetic. They built magnificent palaces and mosques wherever they went, including the Dome of the Rock at Jerusalem. This mosque was built on the site of Solomon's temple, which was built by Solomon, the third king of ancient Israel and the son of King David and Bathsheba. Building the new religion's house of worship on the ruins of the conquered people's sacred place of worship was common in ancient times. This showed dominance over all other religions. It was certainly a cruel blow to the Jews, but in other ways, however, the Muslims were tolerant of Christians and Jews and gave them freedom to practice their faith and conduct their own affairs. In fact, Jews and Christians often held positions of power and were recruited into the military.

ABBASID CALIPHATE

In 750, the Abbasid Caliphate took over power from the Umayyads and moved the seat of power from Damascus to Baghdad, in present-day Iraq. The conservative, traditional Abbasids imposed an austere rule that strove to insulate Islam from the "decadent" Western influences at Damascus.

The Umayyads remained powerful in Spain, however, and many Greek-influenced Syrian and Jewish scholars moved to Spain. They brought with them the Greek books that had been lost or forgotten in the "Dark Ages" of Western civilization but still existed in Arabic. In this way, Muslim scholars introduced the works of Aristotle and other Greek scholars to Europe.

THE DECLINE OF SYRIA'S POWER

Syria declined after the shift of power to Baghdad. Then in 877, Syria was made part of Egypt, and culture flourished again from 900 to 1000, an era of great poetic works, often referred to as Syria's Golden Age. This activity centered at Aleppo in the north. Then for the next few hundred years, Greater Syria fell under Turkish domination.

The passionate universality of Islamic faith and law had not resulted in a lessening of traditional rivalries between tribes and families, however. While most Syrians were Muslim, there was no strong central power to unite them as there had been under the Umayyads, or even under the Greeks or Romans. Rivalries, strife, and disorder were widespread in Greater Syria when the first Crusaders arrived from Europe in the eleventh century.

CRUSADERS FROM EUROPE

For quite a long time, there had been a practice of "protection" in Syria. Islamic rulers, like the Greeks and Romans before them, tolerated other religions and tribes, as long as they were obedient, paid their taxes, and posed no direct threats. But minorities were particularly vulnerable to hostile, predatory tribes, so the rulers allowed these minorities to be placed under the "protection" of more powerful groups, who lived elsewhere but could be called on to "settle accounts." Christians who lived in the area and

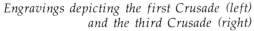

Engravings depicting the first Crusade (left)
and the third Crusade (right)

Westerners who came to Jerusalem and Bethlehem on holy
pilgrimages often needed an escort of Western armies.

However, the ruler then in power in Jerusalem in the eleventh
century decided to forbid pilgrims from Europe to enter
Jerusalem. This outraged devout European Christians who held
Jerusalem sacred and considered they had a right to worship
there. So they sent soldiers to reestablish access to Jerusalem by
force.

For reasons that scholars have debated for a long time, the cause
of liberating Jerusalem became very popular in Europe. Perhaps
the rulers chose to use the situation to rally different warring
factions against a common enemy, or perhaps they wished to give
moral credence to their reign by leading a holy war. Certainly,
medieval morality emphasized struggles between good and evil.
Later on, however, after the Crusaders had spent time in the

The Castle of the Knights built by the Crusaders

Middle East, they began to be aware of the riches there, and their motives became less pure.

The Muslims had similar reasons for fighting. The disunited, quarreling tribes closed ranks in a cause against a common enemy. And they had an exceptionally strong leader—Saladin, a warrior and the Muslim ruler of Egypt. By all accounts, he was a gifted, noble leader who embodied high moral principles with the same code of chivalry and honor as the Europeans, who were led by Richard the Lion-Hearted. For the Muslims, the Europeans were the "infidels" and the Muslims were the "crusaders."

There were three Crusades: The first in about 1099, when Europeans gained Jerusalem; during the second, they lost the area to Saladin; and in the third regained it, although their control was much weakened. They built a castle, established a kingdom, and settled the area from the Syrian coast to Palestine, but were unable to keep the area effectively.

Left: Saladin
Above: The Turks capture Constantinople.

This was an extremely short period in history, but it made a very large impact on European and Arab cultures. For Muslims, resentment of the presumptions of Europeans regarding this territory would continue and deepen over time.

SALADIN

The reign of Saladin in the late twelfth century created a united Egyptian-Syrian kingdom, the Ayyubid Caliphate. Saladin captured Jerusalem in 1187 and extended his rule northward to include Damascus and Aleppo.

MAMELUKES OF EGYPT

But for the next few hundred years Syria was in turn under the rule of the Mamelukes of Egypt and various northern tribes. Tamarlane the Mongol sacked Aleppo and Damascus, taking away not just wealth, but many people, including almost all the skilled tradesmen.

OTTOMAN TURKS—A FOUR-HUNDRED-YEAR REIGN

In 1516, Turks conquered Syria and held it for four hundred years. The long, illustrious reign of the Ottoman Empire (called Ottoman because of the founder of the dynasty, Osman or Othman) was most dynamic at the beginning, but degraded into weakness and disorganization at the end. The Ottomans were cruel to those who opposed them, but to the obedient, Ottoman rule could be comfortable and efficient. They greatly improved agricultural methods in Syria and this led to prosperity. They imposed order, new laws, and most of all, taxes. Syrians were allowed a great measure of autonomy and could live according to the laws and customs of their individual communities. This applied to Christians and Jews, too, although they were taxed more heavily than Muslims.

Jews and Christians and some other groups were allowed a measure of freedom to rule their own people. Under a system called the *millet*, religious courts could make, judge, and enforce certain of their own laws on their own people—provided, of course, these laws did not impinge on other groups. These courts had domain mostly over matters of marriage, divorce, birth, inheritance, dietary laws, and sometimes even punishing thieves and murderers. This custom existed up to the end of the Ottoman Empire, and even today the bedouin are allowed their own laws and courts.

Because of new sea routes found to India late in the sixteenth century, Syria was no longer an important East-West trade route.

EUROPEAN INFLUENCE

By the sixteenth and seventeenth centuries, Syria's relations with France and England had grown very strong. It was mostly the Syrian Christians and Jews who engaged in trade with Europe (Syrian Christians had always had ties to Europe, first to Greece in ancient times and then to Italy in the Renaissance), and they were growing rich. Because the French traveled there often, they established Catholic missions, as well as Eastern-Christian rite, European schools. Aleppo, as well as Lebanon to the south (which was then part of Syria), was a center of this trade and European influence. This economic and cultural cross-fertilization enriched Muslim thought and had a great effect on Europeans, too.

It was increasingly difficult for the Ottoman Empire to maintain its huge empire efficiently. In 1831, the Egyptians took over Syria, but the Ottomans won it back with the support of the Europeans.

European goods had been flooding the market, replacing Syrian products, and the merchants who were importing these European goods were Syrian Jews and Christians. Resentment over the European presence that enriched Christians and Jews to the detriment of Muslims resulted in often violent conflict between Druzes and Maronite Christians in Lebanon.

STIRRINGS OF NATIONALISM

In 1789, the French revolution took place. As a wave of nationalism and revolution spread with Napoleon Bonaparte across Europe, Syrian and Middle Eastern intellectuals began to feel its impact, too. The Syrians affected were a very small group to begin with, but the seeds of nationalism and independence were

Turkish soldiers in Damascus during World War I

planted, and they would grow slowly and steadily.

Meanwhile, the Turks had commissioned French companies to build railways and telegraphs, which improved the economy greatly and changed ways of life and work. Cities such as Aleppo and Damascus showed growing Western influence in clothes and customs, and Western schools became fashionable. The American University was established in Beirut by American Protestants in 1866.

Even though Arabic-speaking Syria was ruled by Turkish foreigners, most Syrians accepted the Ottoman rule because the Turks were fellow Muslims, if not fellow Arabs, and ruled according to Islamic law.

THE ROAD TO INDEPENDENCE

In World War I, the Turks entered into an alliance with Germany, and Syria and the Middle East became a battlefield with Germans and Turks on one side and French and British on the

The League of Nations divided Greater Syria into four states after World War I (left) and the French (right) took over Syria.

other. Syria and other Arabs helped the British and revolted against the Turks. In return, Britain was to help support the Arabs in their quest for independence.

Britain's main interest was to control the Suez Canal in Egypt, which gave them access to their colonial empire. On the other hand, the French were interested in the well-being of the Catholics in Lebanon. Britain and France, in the Sykes-Picot Agreement of 1916, divided the Ottoman territories between them. Britain would take the southern two-thirds of Iraq. Coastal Syria and Lebanon south to the present-day Lebanon-Israel border would go to France. The rest of the land would be independent Arab states, but Britain would have "special rights" in the southern section, and France in the northern part.

With the defeat of Germany and the end of World War I, Greater Syria was divided by the League of Nations into four states: Lebanon, Palestine, Syria, and Transjordan.

THE FRENCH MANDATE

The French government was given control over Syrian affairs. This period, starting in 1920, is called the French Mandate, and the division of land was similar to that outlined in the Sykes-Picot Agreement.

Syria was divided into administrative regions. The Alawites and Druzes made up separate areas. Aleppo and Damascus also were separate states. This further segregrated the Alawites and Druzes from the Sunni majority.

The French helped to advance Syria; they built much-needed roads and established the Arabic-language University of Damascus. But they were slow to give up power. For one thing, they wanted the Lebanese Christians to be safe when they left. The long tradition of protection was still prevailing.

The Arabs, however, continued to ask for self-government. A treaty was drafted in 1936 between Syria and France for Syria's independence. But Turkey, who was afraid Syrian Arabs would gain control, convinced France to give the Turks an important role in the territory. So the 1936 treaty never was realized.

WORLD WAR II

In 1940 France fell to Germany. This encouraged the Syrians to strive harder for independence. In 1941, Germany sent aircraft to Syria. Immediately the British and Free French armed forces invaded and occupied Syria and Lebanon. At the end of the war, the Free French announced Syria and Lebanon independent, but the French government delayed. Finally the last French forces left on May 17, 1946. This date, called "Evacuation Day," marks Syria's independence. Lebanon also gained independence in 1946.

Chapter 6

AN INDEPENDENT
NATION

After gaining independence, many semi-autonomous groups and warring factions struggled for power. There were the wealthy, the poor, the townspeople, the nomads, the educated, and the illiterate. There were Communists and Socialists. There also were different religious groups, Christians and Muslims. The Sunni Muslims were the majority; the Alawites, Druzes, and Shiites were minority groups. All were struggling to have their voices heard and the country suffered from political instability.

At first Sunni landowners took power, but they could not unify the country. Shukri al-Kuwatli became head of the civilian government. But in March 1949, a military coup toppled Kuwatli and two more coups followed in the same year.

Colonel Adib Shishakli assumed power after the third coup and the military gained an important role in governing the country. But in 1954, the military was in turn ousted and the country was returned to civilian rule.

THE UNITED ARAB REPUBLIC

In Egypt in the 1950s, President Gamal Abdul Nasser led an Arab nationalist movement that gained many supporters in Syria.

Raising the Syrian flag in 1961

Under the instigation of Syria's political leadership, Egypt and Syria formed a country called the United Arab Republic (UAR) in 1958. This arrangement worked to Egypt's benefit and Syria's detriment, and ended with a coup in 1961. This experiment in Arab unity was a great disillusionment for Syrians, and thereafter, no matter how much passionate rhetoric they produced on the subject of Arabic solidarity (and against Israel and the West), they would shrewdly and pragmatically act in their own national interests and not seek union with other states.

THE BAATH PARTY

During World War II, the beginnings of a new political party to promote pan-Arab unity started. It was the Baath party and called itself the party of the masses. But it gained members from the educated, civil servants, soldiers, and professional men. Its beliefs in pan-Arabism and social rights attracted many students. By the 1950s, more people were being drawn to the Baath party.

THE BAATH PARTY AND PRESIDENT ASSAD

The Baath party had branches in Iraq, Lebanon, Jordan, and elsewhere, with a central committee that had influence over party activities in Syria. This international party is similar to the Communist party structure, where the party in the Soviet Union has a role in directing parties in other Communist bloc countries. But the Baathists were anti-Communist and very nationalistic.

In 1963, Baathist officers seized power in Syria. The leaders were mainly Alawites and Druzes who wanted to help the less advantaged with land reform and other changes in the economy. Many of the wealthy families were exiled and their property seized. The country's policies moved decidedly to the left and the Baath party concentrated on developing the countryside.

The next few years were difficult. Disagreements occurred in the Baath party leadership. In 1970, a member of the military, Hafez al-Assad staged a bloodless coup and soon became president. This aroused protests from many Sunnis, because in addition to being a Baathist, he was a minority Alawite. Assad was nonetheless able to hold the country together very well. (He was reelected in 1978 and again in 1985 for additional seven-year terms.)

Since Syria achieved its independence in 1946, its government had been marked by instability in the ensuing decades. Numerous governments were installed in office and then removed, generally following military coups. This process came to a halt with the accession to power of President Assad, a strong and determined leader. He controls the various governmental institutions, directly or indirectly, as well as the Baath party and the military. No significant decision is taken in Syria without his explicit or tacit approval.

President Hafez al-Assad

PRESIDENT HAFEZ AL-ASSAD

Assad was born into the Matawirah tribe in Qardahah, in the Jabal an Nusayriyah of Latakia Province in 1930. This isolated mountain stronghold of the Alawite is a very poor region. Most Alawites were poor farmers, working on land owned by absentee Sunni landlords. Most official positions were hereditary and passed on to other Sunnis. Alawites had little opportunity in this Sunni-dominated society. Other than farming, the only way that talented Alawites could get ahead was to join the armed forces. As the new Syrian armed forces grew, more Alawites joined. The ambitious ones found many opportunities, and were promoted quickly, becoming a very powerful majority in the officer ranks of the military. Assad entered the air force college in 1952, served as a jet fighter pilot, and by 1964 he was commander of the air force. This is how Assad came to prominence and power in Syria—as a powerful commander with a loyal group of fellow Alawite officers and troops behind him. Assad was a strong Socialist and supporter of the Baath party. Like the other Alawite officers, he was grateful for the opportunities for advancement that Socialism provided.

In 1966 Assad became minister of defense. In 1970, with the support of the military, he took control of the country in a bloodless military coup. He proved an effective leader and was later elected president in a popular election.

Assad has ruled with a combination of efficiency, charm, and military power. He has known periods of high popularity, but he also has been severely criticized. He and his party have a great many enemies both on the right and the left. The many wealthy and powerful landowners do not appreciate the loss of privileges they enjoyed in the past. And there are many Muslim extremists who resent the Alawite rule.

In 1982 a group of Alawite army cadets were assassinated by Islamic fundamentalists known as the Muslim Brotherhood. In retaliation Assad sent troops to the Syrian city of Hama, where the Islamic fundamentalists had been engaging in open rebellion. As many as twenty-two thousand people were killed. Assad was severely criticized for this mass slaughter. But order was restored, and many critics came to appreciate his ability to maintain order.

Assad has great influence in the Middle East and most diplomats and Middle East experts believe that Syria must play an important role in any comprehensive Middle East settlement. Assad has been a key player in keeping peace in Lebanon—and creating havoc in Israel.

MIDDLE EAST CONFLICTS

Massive internal and external strife came with independence in 1946. Internally, various factions struggled for power, and many

Israelis celebrate their independence.

coups took place. Externally, there were conflicts with other Arab states. But the most important conflict was with Israel. To all Arabs, the Israelis are a symbol of the foreign domination and imperialism from which they struggled to free themselves. They resent the displacement of Palestinian Arabs from Palestine, much of which is in the area that is now Israel.

THE CREATION OF ISRAEL

The state of Israel was created around the same time that Syria became an independent state. For both countries, the seeds of nationalism had been begun long before then. It was a long, slow process in both cases. The official independence dates are April 17, 1946 for Syria, the date they routed the French, and May 14, 1948 for Israel, the day they declared themselves independent from the British at the termination of the Mandate.

As long ago as 1917, the British had promised Jews a "national home" in Palestine, which was then to come under British domination. This document was called the Balfour Declaration. But the declaration also noted that the civic and religious rights of the Palestinians would not be affected.

Jews in Europe, particularly, were enthusiastic about the creation of a homeland in Israel, the first they had known in thousands of years. Some began to settle in this area, often buying land. This was a slow process, but it made the indigenous Arabs of Palestine uneasy.

Then in 1947, after World War II and the knowledge of the Holocaust, world sympathies were strong for the creation of a homeland for the Jews, particularly for the many refugees created by the war. In 1947 the United Nations General Assembly passed a resolution calling for the partition of Palestine into Jewish and Arab states. This resulted in riots in Syria and elsewhere in the Arab world. The Arabs felt it was another betrayal, Europeans were once again reneging on promises. Giving up any part of Palestine was intolerable.

WAR BETWEEN THE ARAB STATES AND ISRAEL

The first Arab-Israeli War came immediately after Israel declared its independence. The newly independent Syrian army invaded Israel from the Golan Heights in the north, while other Arab countries invaded Israel at other borders. The goal was to prevent the creation of Israel. This effort resulted in a defeat and humiliation for the Arabs, who found that their strong nationalist passions did not translate into an efficient military machine.

The realization of their shortcomings was all too evident, and there were many shake-ups in governments and the military, with charges of profiteering, cronyism, and widespread criticism of

An Israeli tank during the first Arab-Israeli War

their inability to function as an army. Most important, the courage and abilities of Syrian soldiers were questioned. In contrast, the Israelis, themselves citizens of a new country with many of the same problems, were both more efficient and showed more bravery.

Resentment against Israel redoubled and became more bitter. Skirmishes along the Arab-Israel borders continued sporadically. Eventually they escalated into air and artillery attacks with a continuing pattern of attacks and reprisals. Syria entered into agreements with the Soviet Union for military equipment and training that the Soviet Union was happy to provide as a means of gaining influence in Syria, and to undermine Israel. Militarily they provided much-needed training for Syria's armed forces.

SYRIA, JORDAN, IRAQ, AND EGYPT FIGHT ISRAEL

In 1966 Syria signed a mutual defense pact with Egypt. Eventually, Iraq and Jordan joined this alliance.

Syria had been shelling Israel from their Golan Heights territory—a highly strategic position on the Syria-Israel border,

1,969 feet (600 meters) higher than the territory in Israel. When Iraq and Jordan joined in the alliance, Israel anticipated another full-scale attack, and planned a preemptive strike. On June 5, Israel attacked several major Arab targets, primarily in Egypt. As the war escalated and Jordan, Syria, and Iraq joined in the fighting, Israel captured the Golan Heights, which had endangered their territories for so long.

Besides losing many lives and a strategic territory, thousands of Syrians who inhabited the Golan Heights were forced farther back into Syria. This defeat was even worse than the previous one. It caused a major shake-up in Syrian politics.

THE 1973 WAR

Both Syria and Egypt wanted to regain territories lost to Israel in previous wars. Syria wanted the Golan Heights back. Egypt wanted the Sinai Peninsula. Syria had been receiving aid and arms from the Soviet bloc for some time and felt confident of its military abilities. In a joint effort Egypt and Syria launched a war in October 1973, called the Yom Kippur War by the Israelis and the Ramadan War by the Arabs. They received some military support from Iraq, Jordan, and Morocco and other assistance from other Arab states.

The United Nations intervened and negotiated a cease-fire. Ironically, even though this war was even more destructive to Syria than the 1967 war, it was a source of pride for the Syrians because they made a much better showing as an armed force. They exhibited more individual and collective bravery than before, and Assad was credited with the ability to unite his countrymen.

In May 1974, under the initiative of former United States

Israeli tanks withdrawing from part of the Golan Heights in 1974

Secretary of State Henry Kissinger, an agreement was reached with Israel whereby Syria recovered territories, including a part of the Golan Heights that were lost in 1967.

AID FROM THE UNITED STATES, THE SOVIET UNION, AND ARABS

The United States had been worried about the closeness of Syria and the Soviet Union. In June 1974 during a trip to the Middle East, then United States President Richard Nixon went to Damascus and met with President Assad. Official relations, which were broken off in 1967, were restored, and informal relations improved for a time. In an effort to win Syria's support, or at least to diffuse hostility, the United States recommended a program of foreign aid to Syria, mainly for economic development.

Syria has always depended on foreign countries to fund its ambitious program of development, as well as its army. It received aid from the Soviet Union, the United States, and also from wealthy Arab countries. In 1974, the oil-rich Arab states began giving Syria $1 billion a year, with the express purpose that Syria act vigorously against Israel. With its huge, and by now very efficient, Soviet-trained military, it could be counted on to continue its efforts. This directive might be interpreted to include terrorism, too. In later years, many instances of world terrorism have been traced to Syria, often with Soviet complicity.

LEBANESE CIVIL WAR

A new battleground between Israel and Syria was established in Lebanon as a result of the civil war that began in 1975.

Syrians have strong emotional and practical ties to Lebanon. They regard Lebanon as a part of Syria. The same families or tribes and religious groups are spread out over both countries, particularly along the borders. They are trading partners also.

When conflicts between Christians and Muslims in Lebanon broke out in civil war (agitated by the Palestine Liberation Organization, the PLO), Syria was concerned. While Syria was certainly sympathetic to the Muslims who had been an impoverished underclass in Christian-dominated Lebanon, they did not feel the kind of chaos that resulted from the civil war was healthy for affairs in the region. Furthermore, Syria always had good relations with the Christians both in Lebanon and in Syria.

Syria has been effective in mediating conflicts between the various warring factions in Lebanon, but often force was necessary, too. In 1976 Syria sent military forces to Lebanon to keep peace. Then they sent troops, fighting mainly against PLO guerrillas and Christian militias.

A captured Syrian tank is used by the Israeli army to shell Beirut in 1982.

Israel, too, wanted peace in Lebanon, and certainly did not want a government that would be a threat to them. The Christians in Lebanon had been their allies, and they wished to protect them, as well as to help institute a moderate government. Israel entered Lebanon to enforce truces that had been made; they too fought the PLO, but helped the Christians. The main goal was to ensure that the PLO would not use Lebanon as a base for military or terrorist operations against Israel.

Not surprisingly, in 1982, Israel invaded Lebanon to destroy PLO positions there and Syrian and Israeli forces clashed in eastern Lebanon. The United States mediated a cease-fire and the removal of PLO fighters from Beirut, while Syria backed a group of Palestinian rebels who sought to oust PLO leader Yasser Arafat, thus causing a major rift among Palestinians.

In May 1983, Israel and Lebanon agreed to have all foreign forces removed from Lebanon, but Syria opposed this and the agreement was undone.

Anwar Sadat, Jimmy Carter, and Menachem Begin after the signing of the Camp David Accords

Syria has had troops in Lebanon since 1976 in an effort to keep peace and it clearly has great power to influence the government, as well as the various factions. But Lebanon still lives in tumult and uncertainty. The exact division of population is in dispute, but it is believed that some 40 percent of the Lebanese are Christians and some 60 percent Muslims. Forty percent or more of the Muslims are Shiites, mostly living in southern Lebanon near the border with Israel. Among the Shiites there are strong contingents of militant Shiites with close connections to Iran, who have been responsible for many of the kidnappings of Americans and Europeans as well as other terrorist activities.

EGYPT RECOGNIZES ISRAEL

The Arab-Israeli Wars dealt a heavy blow to Egypt in terms of human lives and widespread economic hardship. Egypt felt it had carried most of the burden of the war against Israel, and was war weary. By 1977, Egyptians were ready to explore a future of peace and security. Egypt's President Anwar Sadat met with Israel's Prime Minister Menachem Begin, and with the help of then United States President Jimmy Carter, signed the Camp David Accords in 1978, which led to the Egypt-Israel Peace Treaty of March 1979.

Egypt was the first and, thus far, only Arab country to recognize formally the state of Israel. Syria and other Arab states were furious and broke off relations with Egypt and excluded them from membership in key Arab organizations. In Egypt, the treaty had some popular support, but there were fundamentalist Muslims, whose influence has grown steadily, who believed it was a treasonous act. A few years after Sadat signed the treaty, he was assassinated by Egyptian fundamentalist army officers.

IRAN-IRAQ WAR

Syria has backed Iran in the long territorial war between Iran and Iraq that began in 1980. Syria maintained that Iraq started the war, but it also wished to support the enemy (Iran) of its enemy, Iraq. Iraq's President Saddam Hussein and Syria's Assad have fought bitterly over control of the Baath Socialist party, which operates in both countries. Syria has accused Iraq of sheltering the Muslim Brotherhood, a militant Sunni Muslim fundamentalist group that is opposed to nonreligious (non-Muslim) Socialist governments, and has fought vigorously to undermine Assad's power in his own country, often using violent means.

Syria was the only Arab country in the region to support Iran, and Iran rewarded Syria by selling its oil at low prices. Syria, in turn, shut down the Iraqi oil pipeline that runs through Syria to a port on the Mediterranean Sea.

In 1987, however, other Arab countries persuaded Syria to join them in condemning Iran, and there was a shaky conciliation of Hussein and Assad. At this time, also, in a renewed effort at pan-Arabic unity, the countries of the Arab League reestablished relations with Egypt.

SYRIA AND TERRORISM

Over the years, there have been numerous instances where terrorist acts were traced to Syria. That Syria supports and facilitates terrorism against Israel and pro-Israeli countries was strongly believed although sometimes hard to prove.

Most of the terrorism and kidnappings in Lebanon have been carried out by fanatical Shiite groups inspired by Iran's Ayatollah Khomeini and affiliated with the Iranian Revolutionary Guards. These groups are based in the Bekaa valley of Lebanon, which is under strict Syrian control. It is doubtful that they could operate effectively without some complicity from the Syrians. However there have been clashes between Iranian guards and Syrian troops.

Sometimes there was overt proof of Syrian activity with terrorists. In 1986, a Palestinian terrorist captured in England, Nezar Hindawi, admitted that Syrians helped plan his attempt to place a bomb aboard an Israeli passenger plane going from England to Israel. He said the Syrians supplied him with a passport and the Czech-made explosives. Syria denied this and other accusations of involvement in terrorist attacks. But Britain had strong evidence of complicity and broke off relations with Syria as a result.

Later in 1986, three Palestinians were convicted of terrorist

A disco bombing in West Berlin, in 1986, was linked to Syrian terrorism.

bombings in West Berlin. The presiding judge announced that the Palestinians admitted getting their explosives from the Syrian Embassy in East Berlin. The judge pronounced that "The court is satisfied that the Syrian link is proven." Consequently, Syrian diplomats were expelled from West Germany.

LAWS AND GOVERNMENT

The constitution states that the laws of Syria must be founded on Islamic law and practice. Islamic laws do not cover all the areas that need legislation and when Syria became independent, they kept the mixture of laws that had been the practice under the long Ottoman rule and the recent French Mandate. Laws reflecting Islamic practice and Socialist goals were added.

The Syrian government is divided into an executive branch under a president elected by popular vote and a legislative body also elected by the people. There also is an independent judiciary, with a Supreme Court above it. The judges are not elected, but appointed by the president. In practice, however, the military government can overrule everyone. The president is also actually a member of the Supreme Court himself. The constitution gives the president strong powers.

POLITICAL PARTIES

Syrians are very interested in politics, both local and Arab world politics. They are also very critical of leaders. But they are not "joiners" or "doers." Membership in official political parties is always low. For centuries, Syrians were unable to participate in government. So the concept of democracy, where they may participate directly, is hard for Syrians to accept and practice.

The party that has ruled Syria since 1966 is the Baath party. It is a Socialist party that took power under a military coup and has kept power by military means. If Syrians do not care to join political parties, they particularly do not want to join Socialist or Communist parties. Membership in the ruling Baath party is low, and membership in the Communist party is even lower. But these parties, although small, are very vocal and have influence in shaping policies. Although not wanting to join the Baath party, Syrians seem to be content to let them rule.

Syrians do join various labor, farm, and professional unions and various groups based on family and religious ties, and they struggle within those groups for dominance. There also are parties, or "brotherhoods," associated with religious groups that have vigorous political goals and are often ready to use violence to achieve their ends.

Chapter 7

MODERN SYRIA—THE ECONOMY AND FUTURE

DREAMS OF THE FUTURE AND THE REALITY OF THE PRESENT

Since independence, Syria has gone through several periods of change and adaptation. The process of becoming a nation did not happen overnight; it was a long, arduous process, starting in the nineteenth century. Syrians had a long time to consider the kind of country they wanted for the future. Like most Third World countries who became independent in the twentieth century, they had a dream of taking their place as equals in the modern world. Ideally, they dreamt of finding a measure of their former glories in ancient times. But in any event, on a practical level, Syrians knew it was necessary for their survival to modernize as quickly as possible, and that usually meant to industrialize.

Under foreign rulers, Syria was neglected. The country often was little more than an afterthought in their plans. Turkey, Britain, and France in turn put their own countries' welfare first, treating their colonial possessions primarily as sources of profit for the parent country. Turkey taxed Syria heavily; Britain and France took natural resources. On the other hand, these countries had supplied a certain security, stability, and guidance (often technological, as when France built railroads and a telegraph system).

If the newly independent countries were to survive without the "protection" of their former rulers, they had to become strong quickly. If they were seen as too weak or disorganized, they risked becoming prey for new foreign conquest and being swallowed up by yet another foreign power.

For many Syrians educated in the West, modernization and industrialization meant erasing entirely and swiftly the old-fashioned past and emulating modern ways completely. Sometimes, people were ashamed of the old ways—the typical Arab styles. In the beginning, these people represented the majority and they were often leftists. A minority were Communists who advocated radical revolution and had no use for religion. Others were politically conservative and religious and had no intention of changing their traditional ways. Gradually, the many Syrians who had adopted modern European life-styles began to be disillusioned. They found Western ways less satisfying, particularly in the context of the Middle East. Their pride in being Syrian grew as they rediscovered the wisdom of their ancestors.

In very many respects, Syrian society was the same as it was in medieval times. Although Syria's city dwellers had acquired European dress and ideas, in the countryside things had not changed too much. Social organization, agricultural methods, and the condition of women were as if time had stood still, and illiteracy was widespread. Centuries of adaptation to survival on a

A dam in the Euphrates River (left), built by the government, has created u reservoir for irrigation. A vegetable stall in the market in Damascus (right) is an example of private enterprise.

difficult land required a nomadic and pastoral life-style where modern ideas were irrelevant.

THE ECONOMY

The government of Syria has been Socialist since 1958. As such, it has been easily able to control the economy and institute land reforms. The Syrian economy is a mixture of government control and private ownership. The larger industries have been government-owned or run, while smaller businesses are privately owned. Key industries such as oil, the railroads, electrical plants, and various large manufacturing enterprises are nationalized. In addition to owning and running key industries, the government also regulates all private businesses. Most farms are privately owned, but there are some cooperatives.

*A donkey used to power an irrigation system (left)
and a tractor (right) working on a mechanized farm*

LAND REFORM

For quite a long time, most of the land, particularly farmland,
was owned by a small number of wealthy absentee landlords who
were not actively involved in farming. Paid laborers and
sharecroppers rarely owned the land they worked and lived on.
By 1958, the new government began to set limits on the size of
land any one person or family could own. This insured that
sharecroppers would get a better share of the crops.

In 1963, the Baath government ruled that anyone who owned
too large a tract of land must sell it, in five years, to the tenants
and peasants at very reasonable purchase prices. Furthermore,
ways for borrowing this money were set up. People who acquired
land through this arrangement, however, had to reorganize into
state-supervised cooperatives.

This probably made many farmers feel better about the equality
of the new Syria, but many independent-minded Syrian farmers

Olive groves under cultivation in the Eghlab valley

just did not want to join government cooperatives, and preferred to lease land on their own. The cooperatives have not been very productive, but they were an excellent way for the government to educate farmers on more efficient farming methods, such as use of machinery and—most important—crop rotation.

It has long been felt that Syria's fertile land could be better utilized through irrigation and more efficient farming. To augment this, the government has built dams that expanded the fertile farmland.

INDUSTRY

The government's development of industry and the creation of new jobs has been a key factor in raising the average Syrian's standard of living. New industries have been created to refine natural resources. In the past, raw materials were shipped to other countries to be refined and processed. Now Syria refines and

Clockwise from top left: An oil refinery, a power plant, sheep grazing near a fertilizer plant, and women sorting sheep wool for market

processes its own oil, natural gas, raw phosphate (used in soap and various chemical compounds), asphalt, and iron ore. The rocky desert yields various other minerals, such as limestone and sandstone, used in glass manufacturing. There are several salt lakes in the north and table salt is extracted from them. Syria's universities have been able to produce all the chemical and industrial engineers that are needed in these industries.

OIL

While Syria is not nearly as rich in oil as some other oil-producing countries in the region, the oil fields in the northeast have helped its economy considerably. Because the oil found in Syria has a high sulfur content, Syria also imports different quality crude oil to blend with its own oil. Refineries are located at Homs and Banias, on the coast.

OTHER NATURAL RESOURCES

In addition to oil, natural gas, iron ore, asphalt, and phosphates are found in Syria.

AGRO-INDUSTRY

Fruit and vegetable canneries produce a significant export. Cotton was and is a good cash crop. Cultivation has been improved and textile manufacturing plants have been established. Wool from sheep pastured throughout the country is abundant and is exported. Silkworms are raised in the north and silk fabric is manufactured in Latakia.

*Copper and brass ware exhibit
the fine work of Syrian craftsmen.*

CRAFTS

The fine handwork that has been associated with Syria is not as
abundant as in the past. Even Syrians themselves prefer cheaper
manufactured goods. Nonetheless, the tradition continues with
the manufacture and export of handicrafts such as brass and
copper work, gold and silver, woodworking, mother-of-pearl
inlays, *damask* steel blades and knives, and damask silk brocade. In
fabric, damask refers to the distinctive pattern woven into the
fabric, which originated in Damascus. In steel it refers to the
Damascus method of welding iron and steel in waved, etched, or
inlaid, decorative lines.

HUMAN RESOURCES

The most important "natural" resource of any country is its
people. Their effect on the economy is at least as important as the

Left: The interior of a rural Arab home
Right: Children in a park in Damascus

land, the climate, or the political structure. Surely, it is a credit to the Syrians that they have been able to survive so well in such a harsh land. Syrians have been traditionally resourceful and tenacious, but as many scholars have pointed out, it is very difficult for a people to fully develop sophisticated skills and talents when all their energies are consumed with basic survival.

Syria's position on the rich trade routes encouraged Syrians to develop skills in trade. This traditional strength exists to this day. Most Syrians are skilled in commerce and trade and ingenious in making money. They are self-reliant and have a great deal of initiative in matters of commerce. When they understand the potential for gain, they also have been quite flexible in adopting new farming methods.

The essential, traditional weaknesses of the Syrians are quite the same qualities, actually, that makes them strong. Their self-reliance or independence makes it difficult for them to work as a team (other than their own natural family, of course). They

A Syrian father and his child

simply do not have a great deal of feelings, trust, or respect for people outside the family. This results in the attitude that they do not owe "strangers" their hard work, loyalty, or sometimes even their honesty. But in relation to their family or clan, their virtue and honesty is complete, and a point of deep pride. Thus, they make poor employees, particularly in the government, even if they are paid a high salary.

Old ways die hard, and many Syrians are trying to change their ways for the good of the country and they are getting used to expanding their loyalties, but this lack of trust is still a problem area.

These attitudes often had catastrophic consequences in Syria's early days of independence, especially in the armed forces. Syrians felt (rightly) that early military defeats were due to their lack of cohesiveness. Their loyalty to their small community served them well under long periods of foreign domination, but in modern times it has resulted in self-seeking graft and a lack of seriousness about one's work. Government-owned and operated industries are looked on as opportunities to enrich the family coffers and provide employment for brothers, uncles, and distant cousins (of which there are very, very many). This leads to enormous inefficiency, and, of course, a snowballing resentment among other Syrians. No one can trust an organization that is overstaffed by the same family members, working for their own personal aims.

THE FUTURE

Syria has few natural resources, and it spends more than it earns. There has been a rapidly increasing problem with a foreign balance of trade (they import more than they export). Syria's economy often has been close to collapse. It counts on foreign aid to survive.

The Syrian form of Socialism is not any more effective, productive, or certainly no more competitive than it is in any other country. Many observers feel that the Syrian government is handicapping its great natural resources—the natural business talents of its people and their individual initiative.

But Assad is committed to a Socialist state. And he has built a power structure backed by a strong, loyal military to enforce his will. In his lifetime, it would be extremely hard to unseat him. His personality has dominated Syria for many years, and when he is eventually no longer president, things are likely to change in Syria. Likely successors would be his younger brother and closest aide Rifaat al-Assad, vice-president for security affairs, or another cabinet member. As head of a feared and often ruthless security

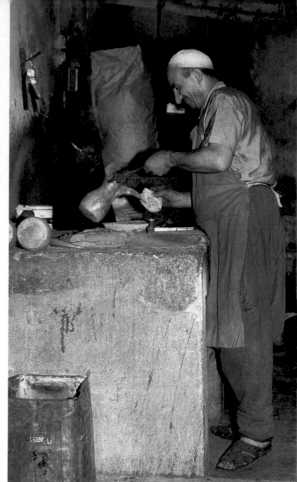

Typical attire worn by the younger generation of Syrians

network, Rifaat Assad has built immense power, which he does not hesitate to use for his own ends (while still being quite loyal to President Assad). Syria would be quite different with Rifaat Assad in power. Considering the network of powerful Alawites throughout the country, it is not likely that a successor to Assad would be anything other than Alawite.

Syrians have made tremendous progress in a short period of time since independence. But their problems are considerable. They seem committed to continuing their war against Israel and supporting the Palestinians, which does not promise a peaceful or a prosperous future.

In the turbulent setting of the Middle East, it is difficult to say what will happen next. Syria seems likely to continue to have its share of problems on many levels, but it has survived five thousand years on a difficult land, experiencing drought, famines, foreign invaders and rulers, and wars and revolutions. Now, with its improved natural and human resources and with strong and stable leadership, Syria is in a position to shape its own destiny and to have an influence in the broader Middle East.

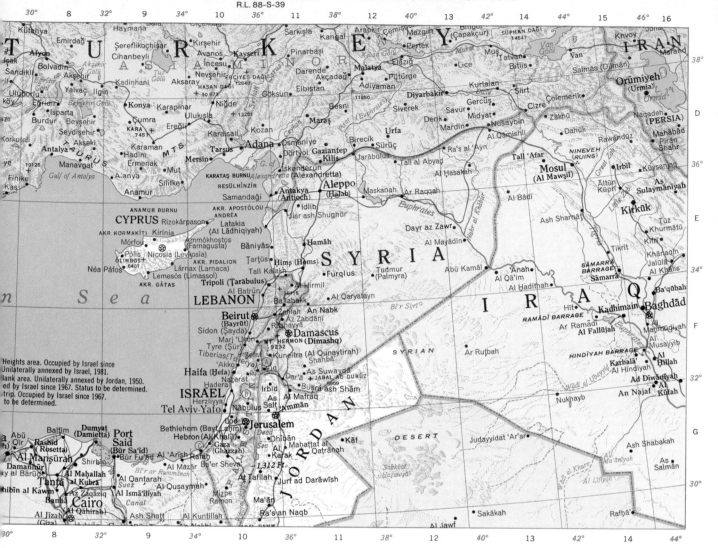

MAP KEY

Abū Kamāl (Abu Kamal)	E13	Damascus (Dimashq)	F11	Latakia (Al Lādhiqīyah)	E10
Al Ḥasakah	D13	Dar'ā (Dar'a)	F11	Maskanah	D12,E12
Al Mayādīn (Al Mayadin)	E13	Dayr az Zawr	E13	Mediterranean Sea	E10
Al Qāmishlī (Al Qamishli)	D13	Euphrates, river	D12,E12,E13	Mokhieba Dam	F10
Al Qaryatayn	E11	Fiq	F10	Mt. Hermon, mountain	F10,F11
Aleppo (Ḥalab)	D11	Furqlus	E11	Nahr al Khābūr (Nahr al Khaubr), river	
An Nabk	E11	Hamāh (Hama)	E11		D12,D13,E13
Ar Raqqah	D12,E12	Ḥimṣ (Homs)	E11	Ra's al 'Ayn	D13
As Suwayda	F11	Idlib	E11	Shahbā (Shahba)	F11
Az Zabdānī (Az Zabdani)	F11	Jabal ad Duruz, mountain	F11	Tall al Abyaḍ	D12
Bāniyās (Baniyas)	E10	Jarabulus	D11	Tall Kalakh	E11
Bi'r Sijrī (Bi'r Sijri), oasis	F12	Jisr ash Shughur	E11	Ṭarṭūs (Tartus)	E11
Busrá ash Shām (Busra ash Sham)		Kuneitra (Al Qunaytirah or el-Qunaytijah)		Tigris, river	D14
	F11		F10	Tudmur (Palmyra)	E12

MINI-FACTS AT A GLANCE

GENERAL INFORMATION

Official Name: Al-Jumhuria Al-Arabia Al-Suria (The Syrian Arab Republic)

Capital: Damascus

Official Language: Arabic. English is widely understood; French, Kurdish, and Armenian are spoken also.

Government: Syria's government is theoretically run by a single political party, but in practice it is controlled by a group of army officers headed by a strong leader. The political system is highly authoritarian, and power is concentrated in the executive branch presided over by the president. The president serves a seven-year term. He is nominated by the Baath party's regional command, and confirmed in a national referendum.

The president appoints the members of the cabinet, the vice-president, and other high officials. He is also commander-in-chief of the armed forces. The cabinet prepares the annual budget, formulates economic plans, and enforces laws and maintains order.

Legislative power is vested in the people's assembly, which is composed of 195 members. Laws show the influence of the long Ottoman rule and the recent French Mandate. They reflect both Islamic practice and Socialist goals.

National Song: "Homat El Diyar" ("Guardians of the Homeland")

Flag: The flag was adopted in 1980. It has red, white, and black stripes with green stars on the white center stripe. The coat of arms shows a hawk, the emblem of the tribe of Muhammad, the founder of Islam.

Money: The basic unit is the pound. In the summer of 1988, approximately 2.54 Syrian pounds equaled one U.S. dollar.

Weights and Measures: Syria uses the metric system.

Population: Over 12 million; 47 percent urban, 53 percent rural

Cities:

Damascus 2,083,000
Aleppo 1,857,000
Homs 790,000
Latakia 234,000
Hama 194,000

(Population based on 1986 Department of State estimates)

Religion: About 86 percent of the people are Muslims. Most belong to the Sunni (Orthodox), but many are members of various Shiite sects, especially the Alawite and Druze.

There is also a sizable Christian minority (about 10 percent), divided into at least a dozen groups. The Greek Orthodox and Armenian Orthodox communities are the largest and most important. Only a few thousand Jews remain in Syria.

GEOGRAPHY

Highest point: Mount Hermon, 9,232 ft. (2,814 m), above sea level

Lowest point: Sea level along the coast

Coastline: 94 mi. (151 km)

Mountains: The Jabal an Nusayriyah mountains run from north to south. They have an average width of 20 mi. (32 km). The Anti-Lebanon Mountains mark Syria's border with Lebanon. Smaller mountains are scattered throughout the country.

Rivers: The Euphrates is the most important water source and the only navigable river in Syria. The Orontes is the principal river of the mountainous region, and its valley is a fertile area for farming. The Yarmuk, a tributary of the Jordan River, forms part of the border with Jordan to the southwest.

Climate: Most of Syria is dry with limited rainfall and a high rate of evaporation. Precipitation occurs mainly in the winter months. Only in the Mediterranean coastal plain and on the eastern slope of the Jabal Ansaryia is precipitation great enough to create a humid condition.

The plain and lower mountain slopes are extremely unpleasant in the summer, when daytime temperatures are in the high 80s° to 90s° F. (30s° to 35° C). Average winter temperatures are in the middle to high 50s° F. (13 to 15° C). In summer the highlands are about 10° F. (5.5° C) cooler than the coast during the day and about 20° F. (11° C) cooler during the night.

Greatest Distances: East to west: 515 mi. (829 km)
North to south: 465 mi. (748 km)

Area: 71,467 sq. mi. (185,180 km²)

NATURE

Trees: Yew, lime, and fir trees grow on the mountain slopes. The date palm is found in the Euphrates valley. Lemon and orange trees grow along the coast. Forests are found in the mountains. Glossy-leaved and thorny drought-resistant shrubs such as myrtle, boxwood, turpentine, arbutus, and wild olive are abundant in the south.

Animals: Wild animal life is sparse. Wolves, hyenas, foxes, badgers, wild boar, and jackals are found in remote areas. Deer, bears, squirrels, martens, and polecats are prevalent. Lizards and chameleons inhabit the desert. Eagles and buzzards inhabit the mountains.

The mule is the beast of burden in the mountains and the camel on the steppe.

EVERYDAY LIFE

Food: The diet of Syrian village peasants consists mainly of bread, rice, beans, yogurt, cheese, olives, and onions, supplemented by vegetables and fruits and by meat on special occasions.

City-based professionals and merchants, however, do have good diets that include more meat. A typical meal might consist of flat bread, meat roasted or broiled with olive oil and lemon, eggplant in a variety of forms, and cheese, dates, or rose marmalade.

Housing: Village houses in northwest Syria are built of mud and straw and are beehive-shaped; those in the south and east are cut from stone blocks. City houses for the wealthy are made of stone.

The middle class live in concrete and cinder-block apartment buildings. Poor urbanites are often squatters on unused land, living in shacks of hammered tin cans or corrugated iron.

Holidays

March 8, Syrian Revolution Day
March 22, Anniversary of formation of the Arab League
April 6, Martyrs Day, memorializing the nation's heroes

April 17, Evacuation Day, commemorating the withdrawal of French troops
November 29, Day of Mourning

Culture: After independence in 1946, a new cultural life began to emerge. The Ministry of Culture and National Guidance has been important in promoting the nation's cultural life.

The National Museum of North Syria at Aleppo displays sculpture, jewelry, and household objects from the Sumerian, Hittite, Assyrian, and Phoenician periods. The National Museum in Damascus has representative treasures from the classical periods of Greek, Hellenistic, Roman, and Arab cultures.

The history of the Christians can be seen in Syria's great churches (mostly in Aleppo) and in shrines. The history of the Crusades is reflected in military fortresses, such as the Crak des Chevaliers west of Homs.

Memorizing and reciting the Koran and poetry are major sources of entertainment. There are still vital oral traditions among nomads and peasants. Two of the finest poets were al-Mutanabbi, who lived in the 900s, and al-Maarri, who lived in the 1000s. During the 900s, al-Farabi became a leading philosopher. During the 1900s, important writers were Omaar Abu-Rishe, Shafiq Jabri, Nizar Kabbani, and Ali Ahmad Said.

Classical Arabic learning lay dormant under Turkish rule. Syrian Socialism was strongly influenced by Michael Aflaq, Salah al-Din, al Bitar, and Akram Hourani.

Kurdish, written in the Latin alphabet, and Armenian are used extensively in modern Syrian writing.

Before World War I, the artistic representation of animal or human life was proscribed by Islam. Figurative art was restricted to geometric designs. Talented artists began to emerge after the war, however. Syrian artists are more concerned with content than with form or style.

Sculpture is mainly confined to decorations hewn in white marble.

The National Theater and other theatrical and folk-dance companies give regular performances.

The Arabic Language Academy, founded in 1919, is the oldest such institution in the world. The University of Damascus is the most important of Syria's cultural centers.

Sports: Soccer, called football, and basketball are very popular, as are wrestling, boxing, tennis, and swimming.

Transportation: Roads are continuing to expand and improve throughout the country. Few Syrians own an automobile.

Railways were not well developed until the 1970s. Two ports, Latakia and Tartus, were built after independence.

There are international airports at Damascus and Aleppo and domestic airports at al Qamishli, Latakia, Dayr az Zawr, and Tudmur. Domestic services are provided by Syrian Arab Airways.

Communication: The government strictly controls all communication media. The press has been subject to direct censorship since 1956. The official Baath party newspaper, *Al Baath*, is one of the leading papers. Radio and television broadcasting are operated by the state-owned Syrian Broadcasting and Television Corporation. Broadcasts are mainly in Arabic, but are also in English, French, Turkish, Hebrew, and German. About 40 percent of the people own a radio and about 2 percent own a television set.

Education: The literacy rate of 64 percent is high for the region. Education is compulsory and free for six years of elementary school. Due to Islamic influence, it is very authoritarian. Enrollment in primary and six-year secondary schools is increasing rapidly. Vocational, teacher-training, and university education are also available. There are universities in Damascus, Aleppo, and Latakia, as well as the Institute of Petroleum at Homs.

The government encourages students to study abroad but discourages the emigration of educated people.

Health and Welfare: Old age, invalidism, and work injury are provided for by law, and health care is free to those who cannot afford private care. Health conditions are generally poor, though they are improving. There is a high incidence of infectious disease in rural areas due to poor water and primitive sewage disposal systems.

Child mortality is quite high and is mostly caused by measles and by diseases of the digestive and respiratory systems.

ECONOMY AND INDUSTRY

Principal Products:
Agriculture: Cotton, wheat, barley, fruits and vegetables, tobacco, sugar beets, livestock
Manufacturing: Textiles, petroleum products, processed foods, cement, glass, soap
Mining: Oil, natural gas, phosphates, asphalt, iron ore

IMPORTANT DATES

3000 B.C. — Nomads settle in area that became known as Syria

1500 B.C. — Aramaens, a Semitic group, establish a strong civilization

1200 B.C.—Hebrews, or Israelites, migrate into southern Syria

538 B.C.—Syria becomes part of the Persian Empire

3rd century B.C.—Persians are conquered by Alexander the Great

64 B.C.—Romans take over the area

A.D. 324—Roman Emperor Constantine begins Christianizing of Roman Empire

632—Islam spreads to Syria after Muhammad's death

635—Arabian armies capture Damascus

661—Umayyad family establishes caliphate with Damascus as its capital

750—Abbasid Caliphate takes power and moves seat of power from Damascus to Badhdad

877—Syria becomes part of Egypt

900-1000—Syria enters a Golden Age, centered at Aleppo

1099—The first Crusade: Crusaders attempt to regain Holy Land from the Muslims

1187—Saladin creates a united Egyptian-Syrian kingdom

1516—Turks conquer Syria

16th and 17th centuries—Syria strengthens ties with France and England

Late 1700s—Seeds of nationalism and independence start to grow in Syria

1831—Egyptians take over Syria

1914-18—World War I; Syrians and other Arabs revolt against Turks

1918—World War I ends; Greater Syria is divided by League of Nations into: Lebanon, Palestine, Syria, and Transjordan

1920—France receives mandate over Syria

1936—Treaty drafted for Syrian independence, but it is never realized

1941 — World War II; British and Free French forces occupy Syria and Lebanon

1946 — French forces leave Syria; Syria gains complete independence

1947 — Syrian and other Arab troops invade Israel

1948 — Israel achieves independence

1949 — Military coup

1958 — Egypt and Syria form United Arab Republic (UAR)

1961 — UAR ends

1963 — Baath party seizes power in Syria

1966 — Syria signs mutual defense pact with Egypt; is joined by Iraq and Jordan

1967 — Israel defeats Syria, Egypt, and Jordan in six-day war; Syria loses Golan Heights

1970 — Hafez al-Assad becomes president in bloodless coup

1973 — Egypt and Syria launch another war against Israel; cease-fire ends the fighting

1974 — Accord with Israel gives Syria back part of the Golan Heights; oil-rich Arab states give Syria massive financial aid

1976 — Syria sends troops to Lebanon in effort to stop civil war there; maintains troops there to keep peace

1978 — Syria angered by Camp David Accords, which led to Egypt-Israel Peace Treaty; Assad reelected president

1980 — Syria backs Iran in war against Iraq

1982 — Assad strikes against Muslim fundamentalists, slaughtering thousands in Hama; Syria and Israeli forces clash in Lebanon

1985   Assad reelected president

1988—Iran and Iraq agree to a cease-fire to end their eight-year war

IMPORTANT PEOPLE

Alexander the Great (356-323 B.C.), conquered many nations, including Syria, from 334 to his death

Yasser Arafat (1929-   ), leader of the Palestine Liberation Organization (PLO)

Hafez al-Assad (1930-   ), became president of Syria, 1971

Rifaat al-Assad, brother of president, vice-president for security affairs

Nueddin Atassi, leftist leader of the Baath party; became president in 1966

Menachem Begin (1913-   ), prime minister of Israel from 1977 to 1983

Constantine (d. 337), expanded the Roman Empire into Byzantium

Al-Farabi (c. 878-c. 950), Muslim philosopher

Hadrian (76-138), Roman emperor

Ayatollah Khomeini (1900-   ), fundamentalist leader of Iran

Shukri al-Kuwatly, became president in 1943, when the military first intruded into politics

T. E. Lawrence (Lawrence of Arabia) (1888-1935), British soldier and author who fought with Syria and Arabs of the Middle East; author of *Seven Pillars of Wisdom*

Al-Maarri (937-1057), Arab poet

Muhammad (c. 570-632), founder and prophet of Islam

Muammar al-Qaddafi (1942-   ), president of Libya; signed pact with Syria in 1980

Anwar Sadat (1918-81), president of Egypt, 1970-81; promoted peace with Israel

Saladin (1137 or 1138-1193), Muslim sultan, considered founder of Ayyubid Caliphate

Adib Shishakli (1909-64), army colonel who overthrew Syrian government in 1949

Suleiman I (1494 or 1495-1566), sultan of the Ottoman Empire

INDEX

Page numbers that appear in boldface type indicate illustrations

About the Author

Margaret Beaton, a native of Chicago, earned her bachelor's degree from Northeastern Illinois University and also did graduate work in French literature at the University of Chicago. She began her career in publishing and advertising.

In 1973, she moved to Paris and worked on the staff of UNESCO, the United Nations Educational, Scientific, and Cultural Organization. For six years, she helped implement programs in education, science, culture, and human rights around the world. The experience of working on an international team, as well as her extensive travel in Europe, Morocco, Egypt, and Kenya, left her with a lively interest in international affairs, and a commitment to furthering goals of international understanding.

After her return to Chicago, Ms. Beaton taught briefly, and since then has worked as a writer and consultant in publishing, direct marketing, and fund-raising.